E-Business for the
Small Business

For Carol, Jonathan, Camilla and Charis

THE SUNDAY TIMES

BUSINESS ENTERPRISE GUIDE

E-Business for the Small Business

JOHN G FISHER

KOGAN
PAGE

First published in 2001

Kogan Page Limited
120 Pentonville Road
London N1 9JN

British Library Cataloguing in Publication Data

A CIP record for this book is available from the British Library.

ISBN 0 7494 3479 1

Typeset by Jean Cussons Typesetting, Diss, Norfolk
Printed and bound in Great Britain by Bell & Bain Ltd, Glasgow

PUT YOUR FOOT DOWN

GET THE FASTEST, MOST RELIABLE OPERATING SYSTEM WE'VE EVER PRODUCED.

Drive your business forward with Microsoft® Windows® 2000 and leave your competition behind. It's 30% faster† and 13 times more reliable* than Microsoft® Windows® 98, and has a range of simplified management tools, helping you save time and improve staff productivity.

And if you really want your competition to eat rubber, why not combine Windows 2000 with Microsoft® Office 2000? With better integration between applications, intelligent new time-saving features and powerful web tools, Office 2000 will help maximise your company's output.

So if you're looking to put your company in pole position, insist on having Windows 2000 and Office 2000 installed on your new PCs today.

To find out more please call **0845 700 1000** ext 2000
visit **www.windowspc.co.uk**, or contact your usual reseller.

Microsoft
Where do you want to go today?®

Contents

Contents

List of advertisers

Business Enterprise Guides

Published in association with *The Sunday Times*
and the Institute of Directors

The Business Enterprise Handbook: A complete guide to achieving profitable growth for all entrepreneurs and SMEs
Colin Barrow, Robert Brown and Liz Clarke

The Business Plan Workbook, Fourth Edition
Colin Barrow, Paul Barrow and Robert Brown

Financial Management for the Small Business, Fifth Edition
Colin Barrow

Starting a Successful Business, Fourth Edition (forthcoming)
Michael J Morris

Successful Marketing for the Small Business: A practical guide, Fifth Edition
Dave Patten

All titles are available from good bookshops. To obtain further information, please contact the publisher at the following address:

Kogan Page Ltd
120 Pentonville Road
London N1 9JN
Tel: 020 7278 0433
Fax: 020 7837 6348
www.kogan-page.co.uk

Acknowledgements

There are so many who helped me put the words together for this book that to thank them all would be another book in itself. For the sake of brevity I list below my main sources of information.

Ask Jeeves, Gary Assim (Shoosmiths), BrandNet, British Venture Capital Association, Business Link, Chartered Institute of Marketing, Aaron Chatterly (XKO Group), Malcolm Davies (Page & Moy Ltd), Deloitte Research, Early Learning Centre, *Executive Intelligence* magazine, First-e, Fletcher Research, Institute of Directors Publications, *Internet.Works* magazine, Jupiter Media Matrix, *Marketing Week* magazine, Jeff Martin (martins-seafresh.co.uk), Microsoft, Ovum Research, PC World, Qualistream, Safeway, Naomi Saunders (Grant Thornton UK), SAS Institute, shopcreator.com, David Stroud (sparesFinder.com), the *Financial Times*, *The Sunday Times*, *The Times*. In particular, grateful thanks to Anna Clores for the manuscript preparation, Helen Driscoll (Freeth Cartwright) for help with legal issues and Andrew Skinner (IGW.net) for constant technical input.

I feel duty bound to urge anyone with serious intentions to get sound, professional advice before embarking on a new e-business, particularly in the area of legal and accounting expertise, as each business situation is different. No responsibility or liability can be accepted by me or any of the professional sources quoted in this book for any loss or damage as a result of the material presented in this brief guide.

The world of e-commerce is moving very fast to the extent that some of the technology or even the sites mentioned as examples may have changed by the time you read this book. So, please be aware that you may need to update your knowledge of what is available now when you come to apply some of the principles mentioned here.

Introduction

Jeff Martin has been in the fishing business for over 30 years. He runs a shop in Newquay with his wife Barbara. Fishing and selling fish to consumers as an independent is a declining trade. EC quotas, dwindling stocks and the involvement of supermarkets in the fish trade make traditional fishmongering a dying art. Profits have been up and down, so much so that Jeff had a short change of career in the 1980s, selling computers for a living.

He was originally an Army engineer by trade and had always been interested in mechanical things. When the Internet became accessible through readily available software packages and cheaper modems, Jeff began in November 1999 to experiment, in his spare time, designing his own Web site from free software. By the summer of 2000 he was recording over 120 visitors a day to his Web site, martins-seafresh.co.uk, and dispatching about 30 orders a week. All the orders were paid for up front using a credit card facility, online. Jeff says it's not a big business compared with the stories you read about in the papers but for the moment it's big enough for him. He reckons he will have to invest in some proper back-office and dispatch systems soon to cope with the rising demand, but it won't replace his shop, as he also has good local business.

The biggest problem, says Jeff, is getting mentioned on the various search engines and having to update the site with the latest prices and availability. Once that is cracked, he should be able to generate around 500 hits a week from UK customers, which would give Jeff enough confidence to employ more staff just to handle the virtual side of his fish business. And then, who knows what the future may bring. (adapted from Hewson, 2000)

E-commerce is destined to become big business, even for small businesses. The recent, much-publicised fall in share prices of dot.com companies reflects more the instability of stock than the commercial opportunity provided by the Internet. Market corrections are inevitable whenever new technology is introduced. Similar falls in value were seen with the introduction of stocks and shares in the railways. But huge growth in the use of the Internet is confidently predicted. Over 35 million businesses will be connected on a global basis through the Internet. Although the United States has around 12 times more computers linked to the Net than its nearest rival, Japan, the UK is the third largest user in the world and the undisputed European leader in its usage of the new technology.

But what is driving this technological phenomenon? Aaron Goldberg, Vice President and Principal Analyst at financiers Ziff-Davis, says:

> The compelling and main reason for e-commerce is simply and ultimately more revenue... it's all about sales. For IT (information technology) this means not just supporting information as it has historically. It's about really supporting sales, so there's an added requirement of a lot of communication among IT, marketing, sales and others. (SAS Institute, 2000)

But the e-revolution is not just about enabling consumers to buy more goods and services direct. Despite the media concentration on retail sales in their coverage of developments on the Internet, less than 1 per cent of all consumer purchases are currently transacted electronically. Everyone agrees that it will grow, but it will grow gradually over many years. Some analysts say that it may well reach a ceiling when it hits 10 per cent or so and stay there. The Internet will be just one of many ways for consumers to buy products in the future.

The real growth area will be in B2B (business to business). By 2004 online B2B revenues will exceed $7 trillion worldwide, representing around 7 per cent of all trade between organisations. Even that may be a conservative estimate. Within Europe, Germany and the UK together will, by 2004, control 46 per cent of all European e-commerce because of their technological capability and business infrastructure. But this time the rewards will not simply go to large companies and the multi-nationals. For the first time, perhaps, in commercial history, smaller businesses are likely to reap the benefits more quickly and more profitably because size, complexity and distribution agreements will, in the future, be much less important than flexibility, dealing direct and tailoring products to a new global market, in the same time it takes to make a local telephone call.

A historic opportunity

Opportunity is one thing. Taking it is another. A recent Europe-wide survey revealed that almost 70 per cent of SMEs (small- and medium-sized businesses) had access to the Internet, but only 30 per cent of retailers and wholesalers and only 17 per cent of manufacturers were using it to generate sales. Even more revealing, less than 7 per cent of those with the Internet could actually carry out online transactions.

The reasons are all understandable. Cost may well be one reason, although in the example given on page 1, fishmonger Jeff Martin reckons he got most of his development work at no cost from the Internet itself by downloading complimentary software. In recent months Jeff has had to pay for positioning on search engines but his total investment, after the cost of his computer and telephone link, was in the hundreds, he claims, rather than the thousands. Security of payment is often mentioned as a potential difficulty too. It isn't, really. Credit card payments are actually more secure online than offline because there is little or no human intervention.

A further worry for some would-be 'e-preneurs' is whether a new Web site will generate too much traffic and create cash flow and fulfilment problems for site owners. But in reality customer build up will be gradual, based on how well the site is marketed, particularly through the most likely search engines – the first places where customers go to find generic suppliers. Another issue is the technical ability to service the site and upgrade the system as needs change. A brief look in any local business directory or on the Internet itself (try www.free-ebd.com) will reveal service providers at all levels of budget or development. Creating and maintaining a Web site need not be expensive; in some cases Web designers are offering to take a small stake in their clients' new e-business in part payment of fees.

Recouping your outlay

It is also a myth to think that e-commerce will always be a drain on the cash of your business and may never make a real profit. That is true of any new venture. But the reality of e-commerce, apart from the much-discussed high profile cash-burners, is that business profits are likely to be available much more quickly than in any comparable, traditional new business venture. If you are converting some of your existing processes to be compatible with online suppliers or to be one step ahead of your competitors, costs are as under control as with any other business investment you make. Many online ideas cost a lot less than you might think.

Consider these examples, taken from Business Link.

Latesail.com

Latesail offers discounts for people who want to charter yachts at the last minute. As each sale is worth between £1,500 and £5,000 it did not take very long to amortise the set-up costs of the Web site and start to make a profit. The initial investment of £10,000 was paid for within three months of launch and enabled Latesail to build up its list of customers who are traditionally very difficult to find with conventional marketing.

Mansfield Motors (Landrover)

Mansfield Motors is a Landrover dealership with a number of overseas customers who need specific parts, as well as good old-fashioned advice.

The company invested around £20,000 in a Web site to service orders on a global basis to over 80 countries as well as offering multilingual versions for certain markets. Its investment paid for itself within six months and the Web site now accounts for over 20 per cent of all parts sales.

Jewellers.net

Traditional jewellers R&J Howarth, based in Bolton, realised that it could use the Internet to widen its marketing within the local area. The initial investment of £10,000 was recouped in the first six months. Web-based revenue now accounts for over 6 per cent of total revenues, with customers from overseas growing strongly, attracted by products not available in their own countries – an unexpected but welcome benefit of going online.
(adapted from Grossman, 2000)

Whether you are an absolute beginner or have already started to trade on the Internet, this book will take you through the steps necessary for building successful and sustainable e-commerce at a profit. Nothing has been assumed and no prior knowledge of computing or the Internet is required. Whenever practical, technical terms will be explained in layman's language to avoid information overload (too much information, provided too quickly).

You do not need to be a high tech business to benefit from the Internet. In fact, the best success stories have been the more traditional businesses that have found new ways to do business by using the basic technology currently available. Local businesses can become national and even global businesses with a few straightforward combinations of hardware (machinery) and software (administration routines) at a surprisingly low cost. Like all new businesses you need to use your common sense and plan for profits on a gradual basis. But unlike traditional businesses the process of building e-commerce profits will differ both in scale and in the type of markets available. The more aware you are of what is likely to happen with your new e-commerce venture, the more sensible your decisions will be, as it grows and develops.

Welcome to the Web.

1 *What is e-commerce?*

The Web and the Internet (short for International Network) are acceler-
ating the transformation of enterprises, both large and small, into globe-
spanning, market-facing enterprises, even as these same firms
ceaselessly confront (whether they like it or not) the competitive realities
of constant, universal access to the global marketplace. (Papows, 1999)
Jeff Papows, President and CEO of Lotus Development Corporation

All businesses exist because they serve a market. Successful enterprises, big or small, keep their customers by providing what they need.
In a traditional business that means knowing your market, buying in
the necessary raw components, combining them in your own unique
way, pricing products to suit the market and distributing them
efficiently. The final element is collecting the money. All of these
stages take time to get right, not to mention boundless energy. Unless
you are very lucky indeed most traditional businesses take up to three
years to show a profit on the bottom line.

What the new technology has done is to solve, for some businesses,
two basic issues which until now have been major causes of early
failure: cash flow and distribution. Using the Internet as your
shopfront, you can ask for the money before you dispatch any goods
or services to customers, thereby reducing your exposure. In some
cases you may not even need to produce the product until an order
is received. The second main benefit of a Web site is being able to
reach potential customers on a global basis with very little marketing

cost. This makes your break-even model completely different from making profits in a traditional business. You could be profitable within a few months rather than having to wait for a couple of years or more.

But e-commerce is also about the back end of the business. The side benefits of installing linked PCs, whether they are all hooked up to the Internet or not, include a more efficient business in terms of dealing with enquiries, product data and pricing issues. These benefits extend back into your relationship with your suppliers, in other words, procurement and debt collection. If your suppliers are themselves on the Internet, even better. At the very least you will no longer need to write letters or send confirmations by mail for agreement. Just imagine how much time that would save for the average business. Linking your staff together using a company-wide 'intranet' (people sending each other messages on a private, company-only system) would abolish the wasteful practice of internal paper memos at a stroke. Decision making right across the company would be improved both in its speed and the discussion of any relevant issues.

Whenever you need to do some research, the Internet can provide access to information and market data which until now has only been available to big companies with big resources and big margins or to members of expensive trade associations. National statistics, trade trends, other people's prices and terms, new products, impending legislation, competitor details are all available, often at little or no cost. All you need is a little patience and skill in knowing how to search out such information on publicly available and often free Web sites.

History of the Internet

The Internet did not suddenly come into being overnight. The system has been in development in one form or another for more than 35 years. Understanding how it all started provides current users with a better appreciation of what it can do.

Let's start by providing a short historical overview of how the Internet was developed and how it came to be widely available so quickly.

When did it all start?

The US Department of Defense was concerned in the mid-1960s that in the event of a nuclear war the armed forces would not be able to communicate with each other through the usual telephone networks. These networks relied on central control exchanges. Scientists argued that such control exchanges would be the first to be attacked in hostilities and therefore could never be the basis of a secure telecommunications system. So they proposed that new technology should be developed whereby messages could be sent directly from one party to another without having to go through an exchange. Each sending station or 'node' had equal status within the system. Messages would be packaged in electronic parcels and let loose on the network to find their own way to their destination through the most efficient route. If any part of the network were to be destroyed, the message parcel simply found an alternative route.

The principles of the new system were tested in the UK at the National Physical Laboratory in 1968 and then later developed by the Pentagon. The first node was a supercomputer based in UCLA (University of California at Los Angeles) to which four more nodes were linked in 1969. For the first time scientists were able to share computer facilities even though they were in different locations, by exchanging data between the five nodes. By 1972 there were 37 nodes in the network known as ARPAnet (Advanced Research Projects Agency net). The Internet today is largely a development of ARPAnet.

When was e-mail invented?

During the trial periods it was noted that scientists were sending each other personal messages as well as academic data and were exchanging ideas of a less formal nature. The concept of 'e-mail' was born. By the late 1980s the National Science Foundation (NSF), a US federal agency, had taken up the task of developing its own network for some government employees using the technology of the ARPAnet, sending messages via new, higher speed transmission lines. To distinguish whether the sender was an academic or from the government, 'edu' or 'gov' was added to the sender's network address. Later on other codes were developed to distinguish the type of user and were included in their electronic address.

How did the system become available to the wider world?

As other organisations acquired computers that could convert messages into packages to be sent electronically (and receive them back) new commercial networks were developed. It was then a fairly simple idea for some of these organisations to link up to create even wider networks. In time, computers bought for businesses and the home came with the necessary decoding programs to send and receive messages through telephone lines which were in turn linked to other networks through Internet Service Providers (ISPs). It has been estimated that over 200 million people are now connected to the Internet via their nodes (computers) and the numbers are growing each month.

Is the World Wide Web something different?

It can be confusing. The terms 'Internet', 'Net' and 'World Wide Web' are often used to mean the same thing. To be more accurate, the World Wide Web is the multimedia part of the Internet. The Web is the collective name for all the documents on the Internet that can be accessed through programs stored on your computer. These access programs are called Web browsers. In essence, the Web browser converts electronic information from other computers into displayed material that you can read or see. Anyone can create a document and make it available on the

World Wide Web for other computer users to read. This displayed material is known as a Web site.

The importance of the Internet as a business tool

When you are running a business you need to grasp issues quickly if you are going to keep ahead. You may already be wondering from the description above what relevance such a system would have for you in your everyday business life. Let's explore just a few ideas.

E-mail

The Internet provides the facility to send and receive written business messages through the telephone network. If you want you can set up your system to be available to receive messages on a 24-hour basis, which is important if you trade with overseas customers. You may want to place or receive an order late at night or during the weekend. Or you may need a rush order completed to help you meet a deadline for one of your own customers and you've missed the post. E-mail sends the message virtually instantaneously.

Data collection

Almost any type of information can be found on the World Wide Web. If you are not sure where the information is, you can ask Internet companies called 'search engines' to help you find it. If you know the name of the organisation that has the information, you can visit its Web site from the comfort of your own office and print off or store in a file any parts or all of it without having to declare your identity.

Discussion groups

Sometimes in business, you just want to talk to someone who has been through a similar commercial experience so that you can avoid costly errors. Using the Internet you can join 'live' discussions on your computer monitor, often on a worldwide basis, and ask questions about your particular issue. You may want to know if there is a market for your products in a foreign country. Join a USENET group or a newsgroup online and ask those people who actually live there what they think.

Long distance data transfer

You may need to send a 40-page document with complex diagrams to a potential client in another continent. If you mail it, it could take days, possibly weeks to get there and even then there is no guarantee it will arrive in one piece. Using the Internet you can 'attach' the document to an e-mail and your client can print out the document on his or her own computer within seconds. Developments in the speed of data transfer mean that pictures and moving images can be sent by the same method.

The building blocks of e-commerce

Once you have realised the potential savings in time and expense which even average use of the Internet can deliver, you will be keen to get started. The process of getting online is not difficult, but as you will discover, once you are connected you may well have to change the entire way you do business.

Here are just some of the basic steps you will need to take to set up and develop your own e-commerce business:

- buy suitable computers;
- link them together;
- rent an extra telephone line(s);
- choose an ISP and go online;

- create a Web site;
- choose appropriate money collection and security software;
- decide what products you can sell online;
- think through sending products to overseas customers;
- be aware of any legal issues that may result;
- create a marketing strategy and business plan for e-business;
- consider how e-business will affect your existing trade;
- develop your database.

It looks like a simple list. From a mechanical viewpoint, it is. Some experts will tell you that they can get you online within a day, but a Web site is not necessarily an e-business. Each step requires you, as a small business owner, to consider all the alternatives currently available if you want to achieve a profitable and sustainable business. It is not easy. The language suppliers use is often confusing as are the claims of speed, efficiency and suitability for your particular business.

Because the skills to help you develop e-commerce are all relatively new, the costs can vary enormously. Equally, because this way of doing business is so new, no one has all the answers. The advice from both start-ups and established players is to take each stage in sequence. Think through how you need to organise your staff to get the best results. It will be a frustrating as well as a rewarding experience, like all new businesses, so be prepared for some hard work.

Finally, do not be afraid to ask so-called experts to explain what they mean. The computer industry is probably the best example in the world of an industry that likes to cloud the issue. At times the jargon can be overwhelming. So do not suffer in silence. Get your new technology suppliers to explain in simple terms what the new piece of equipment can do specifically for your business. If you do not understand it, you probably won't use it, so the investment will have been wasted. Remember that many so-called e-businesses are often nothing more than direct marketing operations that happen to take customer orders electronically. The vast majority of e-businesses still only use the Internet as a way to get enquiries or orders. You do not have to buy the whole e-package to become a bona fide e-business.

As you grow in confidence, so will your awareness of how products, particularly software, could enhance what you do. Use the Internet itself to ask for opinions and ideas. You'll be amazed how helpful other e-business owners around the world will be when you ask for advice.

2

Getting the right equipment

Reading the newspapers you could be forgiven for thinking that everyone except you is trading online. They all seem to be having earnest discussions with their programmers about 'upgrading their system' to cope with the new world of e-commerce. If you are already one of these fortunate entrepreneurs who has all the kit and is on their way to their first million or more, you may want to skip forward to the next chapter. But for most of us just starting down the road to electronic trading the biggest single hurdle to making that idea become a reality is getting the right equipment.

Even though computers are commonplace these days even in small businesses, they are often still dedicated to a single task, such as keeping accounting records or writing letters. You may have bought your computers and software piecemeal as the business has grown, on the recommendation of a friend or business adviser. Hand in hand with the growth in your hardware you may also have had to deal with new telephone systems, mainly for voice calls but more recently for carrying data, even if that means just for a fax or for collecting sales orders. You have probably also acquired various versions of software which may or may not now do the job they were originally bought to do. Supporting the business in this way, keeping costs in step with sales, could well have continued for years with no real need to become any more sophisticated.

But the Internet has changed all that. Your next purchase of computer equipment, software and even your telephone arrangements will now have electronic commerce implications, whether you like it or not. You may even have to think about changing some of your staff.

Deciding what you need

Technology changes fast. To the computer expert today's equipment is already out of date even before it gets to market. But it is very easy to get caught up in the latest innovations only to find yourself putting off buying anything because it might be out of date in a few months. So, with apologies to anyone reading this in two years' time and wondering why I did not suggest system X or product Y, take the ideas in principle and think about your own business to find the solution that would be right for your new e-business now.

To take that vital step from no computers or just a few computers to an integrated communications system that can do business with a potentially global market you need to ask yourself some simple questions:

- What do I need this equipment to do?
- Does the business need to be online all the time?
- How many staff will be involved in my e-business?
- Am I likely to need more computers in the near future?
- Will I be buying supplies online?

Without knowing anything about computer systems at all, if you have a sound business idea you can probably already imagine what you want the equipment to do for you. For a start, you may have already decided that you only want one or two people to be involved in the establishment of an e-business resource in the early days.

Networked systems

It is likely that you will need several members of staff to have access to the Internet. It is desirable that those people should also be able to send each other electronic messages or get information from a shared file or the Internet at the same time. If so, you will need to think about a 'local area network' otherwise known as a LAN – a typical system is shown in Figure 2.1.

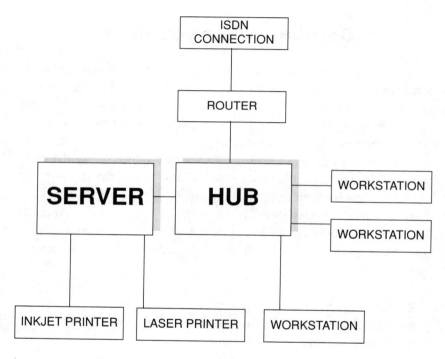

Figure 2.1 Typical LAN system

As you can see from the diagram individual computer terminals are linked together via a hub. The hub receives data from individual users on the system and redistributes the data according to the instructions that come with the data. So, if Sally wants to send a message to Mike electronically, the data travels from her terminal through the hub and is redirected to Mike's terminal. If Jim, the boss, wants to send a message to both Sally and Mike, his data will go to the hub and be distributed to both terminals. Replies are routed back in the same way. Hubs are not necessarily large items of equipment. They could easily sit on a desktop.

Servers and routers

In most companies there are a number of general files that everyone uses from time to time. They could be a list of customers, product information, accounts records or lists of approved suppliers. Often they contain a large amount of historical information which, as paper files, can be bulky and time-consuming to use. The best way to store such records within a network so that everyone can use them easily is to put them into a server or main computer. A server is an electronic filing cabinet that stores the information in an organised way so that individuals at their terminals can retrieve specific items whenever they need them. Because the server has a large memory it reduces the need for individuals to have a large disk capacity in their own computers. When we come to discuss the requirements for individual workstations the need for memory will be an issue if a server is going to be part of your networked system.

Many small businesses already have such systems in place and they work well until the business needs to communicate with the outside world. Traditionally telephones and faxes have done this job. However, as even small businesses have become more complex, especially in the storing of electronic data, the need for separate telephone lines to carry just data has become almost standard. Not only is a separate line more efficient in terms of speed, it also frees up the voice lines so that customers can reach you when they want to. Appearing to be constantly engaged is not good for business.

The problem of freeing up telephone lines is important if you want to expand into e-commerce, as your only link to the Internet will be through a telephone or cable line. But because appliances like telephones work traditionally on an analogue system and data transfer is mostly digital, you will need another piece of technical equipment to 'route' analogue and digital data to the right appliances. A 'router' does this job of providing an interface between your server and incoming data lines. Having got these issues clear in your own mind you will then want to talk to an equipment supplier.

Critical issues when setting up a network

When you come to brief your equipment supplier you may want to bear in mind the following key issues when it setting up a LAN. Whatever the complexity of your needs the following issues are likely to come up for discussion:

- Does everyone in the network need the same equipment?
- Does everyone in the network need different equipment?
- How should the system be wired (floor, ceiling, cabling columns)?
- How should the equipment be connected to the telephone system?
- What level of ongoing technical support will you need?

You may not be able to get definitive answers to these questions before you have decided on what kind of individual computers you intend to buy for your e-commerce team.

Individual workstation systems

The first thing to consider for individual staff is desktop systems that have Internet capability. The package is likely to include a screen, processor, network card (modem, if not installing a LAN), memory, keyboard, mouse and printer – see Figure 2.2.

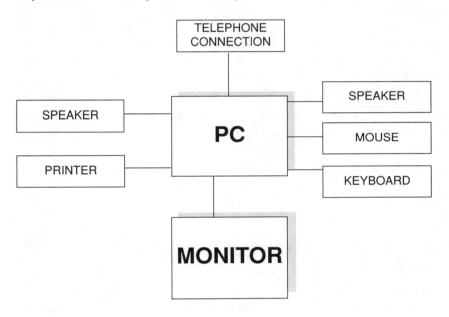

Figure 2.2 Typical workstation

Screens

Over the years visual displays have improved both in size and in graphics capability. Although some commercial communication systems still use small, black and white monitors for listing data such as car parts or industrial products, they are becoming rare. It could be argued that in some industry sectors where all you need is the reference number for a particular item, there's no need to bother to make it colour or use expensive design. The trouble is that software for that reference tool may only be available in colour with graphics the next time it is updated, so you need to consider not only what you want now but also what suppliers will be providing in the years to come.

Screens or monitors are measured in inches by the diagonal size of the tube that displays the image. However, unlike the television industry, which promotes the actual viewable image on the screen, the computer industry does not. Tube monitors have a plastic housing that reduces the actual viewable screen area by around 10 per cent. So, a 15-inch tube monitor, for example, will provide only about 13½ inches of viewable screen. Similarly a 17-inch monitor may well have a viewable image size of less than 15½ inches. When you are considering what size of screen to purchase for your business, always ask to see something on the monitor before you decide. It may well be worth taking one of your 'heavy user' staff along to the showroom to get a second opinion.

Choose an appropriate size of screen

Fourteen-inch screens are no longer available. Fifteen inches is now the most common size of screen but there is a strong argument to consider that 17 inches should now be the industry standard as software and Web designers continue to try and cram as much information into the image area as possible. Mathematically a 17-inch screen is 35 per cent bigger than a 15-inch screen, which offers a big advantage if you want to run more than one program on the screen at the same time, as often happens with customer service queries or purchasing routines. Being able to see what is on the screen clearly will make it easier for staff to use with confidence. Nineteen or even 21-inch screens are still considered a bit of a luxury, but each user will have his or her own profile. A designer or a telesales operative working all day manipulating complex data on screen may well need a 19-inch monitor as standard. The price for a 19-inch screen is currently around 25 per cent higher than the standard 17-inch model.

Go for sharper images

The image on the screen area is determined by the shape of the tiny pixels or dots that make up the image as seen by the user. Tube technology determines the shape of these pixels. Shadow-mask and slot-mask tubes are usually good enough for text-based work. Aperture-grill tubes are better for richer more saturated colouring, which may be a feature required for image-editing or design work, and as such are more expensive.

Another issue to consider is the rate at which the image is renewed or refreshed on the screen. This is known as 'scan frequency'. If the 'refresh speed' is slow users can detect a flicker, which is not only irritating but can lead to chronic headaches and tiredness in some people. A minimum scan frequency of 85Hz is generally recommended to avoid this problem for users who spend many hours a day in front of a screen.

The best screens on the market are flat LCDs. They use lead crystal displays rather than tube technology. They generate less heat and electromagnetic emissions. But their big advantage is their flatness (because there is no tube to house) which saves space in a busy office, and they generally provide a more even picture image. Inexplicably, a 15-inch LCD screen will provide the same viewable area as a 17-inch ordinary tube monitor, so you may want to factor this in to your costings if price is an issue.

Finally, if you know that the screens will be in a sunny position in the office you should check that the screens have been treated with anti-glare or an anti-reflective coating. It's a small issue but one worth watching out for.

Which desktop PC to buy

Whether you have your own office server or not your staff will still need their own desktop system. A PC (or 'personal computer') usually includes the screen, the keyboard, the mouse, the network card and the processor put together as a package for an individual. The processor or central processing unit is the heart of every computer. Its job is to read the software, create the images on the screen and send output data to other devices in the office like printers or indeed other people's computers. It administrates the data.

The main issue with processors for a growing business is what level of sophistication your business needs now and whether your investment will be wasted if you opt for the wrong type of PC. It is true that virtually all PCs can be added to if the user's needs require specific modification, but when you are starting from scratch you should at the very least be able to take advantage of any current technology rather than be upgrading your equipment to do basic business tasks in a few months' time.

The choice of computer may also depend on what software you need to run on it. If you have a piece of specific software that is essential to your industry, your choice of computer may be dictated by the systems that are compatible with it. In addition, if it is a straight choice between two computers you may opt for the one that provides certain types of office software free with the deal.

Processor

There are three main things to consider when buying a PC for business: speed, memory and graphics handling. The speed at which your PC operates depends on the clock speed of the microprocessor, which is measured in MHz (Megahertz). The speed of a current Pentium III processor is 800MHz, but for most business purposes a Pentium II processor would be sufficient, if they are still available. However, if your plan is to use the computer for e-commerce purposes you must also give some thought to the performance of the modem within the

PC, as it is the modem that actually translates data for sending down the telephone line.

Connection speeds

Connection speeds are categorised by 'V' numbers. When you 'hook up', as they say, to the Internet most access routines state at what speed the information is being received. V34 for example is 28,800 bits (units of data) per second. This is now the minimum standard business modem speed you need to read Web site pages efficiently. The next one up, V42, enables you to pick up errors in the data. V90 can support transfer speeds of up to 56,000 bits per second. So, for most SMEs going into e-commerce, V42 or better is what you need.

If you are going to become involved with e-commerce you need to think through your telephone requirements carefully. The telephone system will be your only link with e-customers or other e-businesses, so it is not an area where you can afford to cut corners. In effect your telephone system is your sales channel and needs to be as robust and reliable as any on-the-road sales force or sales presentation systems.

Access to the Internet is clearly the most important issue. Home users can simply link up in the normal way through their PC and a standard telephone line. But an e-business is likely to have more than one Internet user and will probably need to exchange data faster than a home user on a regular basis, simply to be able to communicate effectively with customers and suppliers, thereby taking advantage of the endless source of information which the Web provides.

ISDN

For these reasons an e-business needs to get connected to the Internet using an ISDN (Integrated Services Digital Network) adapter, which would replace a modem. Such systems enable you to exchange data three or four times faster than through a conventional telephone line. There are newer technologies being introduced such as ADSL (Asymmetrical Digital Subscriber Loop) which can send the data through the system even faster. Some commentators say this type of connection will become the standard in a few years' time but to date ISDN is of a guaranteed quality and will do a very good job for SMEs with aspirations in e-commerce.

Leased lines

If you have a global business idea and need to be online 24 hours a day to be able to communicate with customers around the world in different time zones, your business plan may even support leasing a telephone line. A leased line provides a permanent link to the Internet. You pay a quarterly rental rather than for every call you make. You will need to do your sums to decide whether over a full year your business would be better off leasing than paying for each call made. Also, because the connection is always live, you need to consider the implications of better security.

Memory

Memory or the capacity of your PC to store data is your next decision. Most computerised businesses these days use Windows 98, NT or 2000 as their basic software tool for correspondence, data handling and accounting. To use the software efficiently the producer, Microsoft, recommends that your PC has a main memory of at least 32Mb (32 megabytes). However, the reality is that most people will want to use heavy-duty applications like Word and Excel simultaneously, so you can virtually double this requirement to 64Mb, as a minimum. When you look closely at the brochures you may well find that many PCs aimed at the business buyer will have 128Mb memory capacity already installed in anticipation of higher memory needs in the next few years.

You also need to consider what level of hard disk capacity will be required. If the PCs are not linked to a server they will need more hard disk capacity, because the server can store data on behalf of the individual PCs in the network. So, deciding what memory your server will have is a prerequisite before buying your PCs.

Your PCs should have the ability to read CD-ROMs and, if it can be afforded, DVDs (digital versatile disks) as in future data is more likely to be stored on these media than on traditional floppy disks.

Graphics

If seeing images clearly on your screen is a major component of how you want your staff to use the new equipment, you will also have to consider what graphics capability the PC can provide. Reading and displaying graphics are carried out by graphics cards. For most business purposes a 2-D graphics capability is enough to handle basic scrolling and movement, but you might want to consider the 3-D upgrade as many new training and accounting software products now need 3-D capability.

You will be aware when you consider these enhancements that buying a PC for a business can be quite different to buying one for home use, as PCs for entertainment purposes normally require better sound and graphics capability than would be expected for business use.

Mouse and keyboard

A mouse attachment as part of the PC is standard equipment, since speed of operation in business is a key factor. The mouse allows the user to interact with the screen image much more efficiently than using the cursor keys on the main keyboard. The basic mouse is normally attached by a wire and has two panels that are operated by the index finger for the left-hand side and by the second finger for the right-hand side. The left-hand panel moves the cursor to any position on the screen while the right-hand panel can call up specific applications to apply to the text or figures the user is working on.

A common upgrade is for the mouse to have a central panel or wheel so that data can be scrolled or zoomed on the screen without having to press the panel again and again. A further sophistication is a cordless or remote mouse that is not connected by wire but communicates by radio or infrared emissions. Some users find this easier and faster to use than having the mouse attached by cabling.

Keyboards come as part of every PC package but you do not necessarily have to use the one supplied. If your users spend a lot of time at the screen it may be worth considering the more ergonomic keyboard designs available, both to improve typing speeds and make lengthy tasks less tiring. Keyboards can also be cordless if required.

Printer

For e-business purposes, your printer requirements will be the same as for a standard business. If you decide to set up a network you could choose to have one printer for all your PCs as a central resource rather than buying several individual printers of varying specifications. This would enable you to buy a better machine overall to support your new network. Laser printers are now the preferred choice for businesses as the replacement cartridges produce about 6,000 pages of print at a cost of only 1 penny per sheet. Ink-jet printers are more suitable for shorter runs and colour output. Most businesses have both kinds and send relevant work to each type of printer to get maximum efficiency.

Specifying the 'kit'

So to sum up, if you are buying for business use with e-commerce in mind, as a minimum you will probably need a system with the following criteria:

Monitor	**PC**
17 inches or more screen dimension	Pentium II processor
75Hz or more refresh rate	V42 modem speed, or 10bT
Shadow-mask or slot-mask tube	network card
Anti-glare screen treatment	64Mb main memory, or better
	10Gb hard disk memory

Ongoing costs

Unfortunately buying the equipment is not the end of the expense. Such a system will require ongoing support if it is to deliver reliable benefits to your growing business. A recent survey showed that the initial purchase price of equipment to establish a LAN was just 15 per cent of the eventual total support cost over the ensuing five-year period. If you go the local area networking route you will have to consider employing a part-time or even a full-time systems manager just to keep the equipment running smoothly if you do not have reliable support from a local supplier.

Choosing an Internet Service Provider

Now that you have all the equipment and have decided which telephone option to use, you need to get your business connected to the Internet. As you will have already learnt, the World Wide Web is a very democratic system but it has no central controlling body. So when you want to get information from it, something needs to take your message and its attached instruction and direct it to the right destination, wherever it is in the world.

ISPs

Internet Service Providers (ISPs) provide the technology required to re-route electronic messages between Internet users. There are a number of ways this can be achieved. You can rent space on an ISP computer, which will hold whatever details you want to publish on the Web. Such services are sometimes known as virtual servers. Alternatively, you can send data directly on to the Internet from your own server: your Web site on your own server can be linked to the Internet.

Individuals and home users are likely to rent space on an ISP such as AOL or BT Internet for a fixed fee each month if they are using it mostly for e-mail or occasional access to buy goods or obtain information. Budding e-businesses, at least initially, will probably want the ISP to host any data on their computer as this will result in faster download times. To some extent it would also keep your data protected in the event of technical or accidental damage on your own premises.

The second option is to have your own server and communicate directly with potential customers via an ISDN line, but this is relatively costly and would require you to have technical support on site to manage and run it.

Registering your domain name

A contributing factor to the decision as to whether to rent space or have the ISP manage your server is your e-business name, or 'domain name' as it is known.

If Widgets Ltd rents space with an ISP the address will appear as 'widgets@aol.com'. In the commercial arena this could be a little confusing as AOL is also a business in its own right. By asking the ISP to host your server or by buying your own server you will be able to have an address that reads 'enquiries@widgets.co.uk', which would be less confusing for customers. In this way you will be able to establish your own corporate identity online.

If you have an existing traditional business you may want some kind of generic company link for your Web site name so that customers can see it all comes from the same company. Alternatively you may want to distance the new venture entirely to reach a new market. The Prudential Assurance Company has an online banking venture called 'Egg', but the Web site for the online version of the Encyclopaedia Britannica is simply 'www.britannica.com'.

Looking at the end of your domain name you do have a choice depending on your type of organisation and where in the world you are based; current site suffixes are shown in Table 2.1.

If you want to be a 'co.uk' or even a 'ltd.uk' you will need to register your new name with Nominet (www.nic.uk) which is the UK's domain name registration agency. Finding a domain name that has not already

Table 2.1 Examples of site suffixes

Global sites	Country sites	Non-commercial
.com	.uk	.ac or .edu
.net	.fr	.org
.gov	.de	.gov

been taken is not easy. Although registering a domain name with the intention of selling it on to a bona fide user ('cyber squatting') has been outlawed as 'stealing', the legal aspects of what you can and cannot register are worth studying before you get too excited about that special name you have chosen (see Chapter 6, Legal issues and you e-business) You may have to do some creative thinking if you find your favourite name has already been legitimately taken by someone else.

Nominet processes around 200,000 new names each month and acts like Companies' House but for e-businesses in the UK. In basic terms just like with a traditional company, the allocation of new names is on a first-come, first-served basis. The best way to register your e-business name is to ask one of the ISPs to do it for you, such as BTConnect or Internet Central. Costs vary depending on the range of services you wish to use, as connection usually comes as part of a package. They will contact one of the Internet name registration companies like NetNames or NetBenefit. They enter your chosen name so that the system can search to see if it has already been registered. If it has, you will be asked to choose again. A dummy site can be established at your new domain that acts as an e-mail facility until you are ready to have a proper Web site designed.

Some people, for whatever reason, prefer to have '.com' as part of their e-business name as it does suggest a more international outlook. To get a dot.com name you will need to register your name with the

US domain names agency, Internic (www.internic.net). However, fashions change. A recent study by The Henley Centre revealed that e-business names ending in 'co.uk' for UK customers were perceived to be more trusted than those ending in '.com'.

Registration of the name of your new business does not, of course, absolve you from also having to register your company, if it is a new one, with Companies' House. But at least it now has a Web site of its own, www.companieshouse.gov.uk, and you can register online.

Choose your ISP with care

There are hundreds of ISPs to choose from at present. Some free access ISPs are often small, local companies that simply provide an efficient link to the Internet but with no frills. However, you need to be careful. Many ISPs have experimented with offering a 'free' service only to find themselves swamped with enquiries, putting significant strain on the entire customer ISP system as well as their finances, which is bad news for a growing business that would be relying on an ISP to put it in contact with customers.

Ben Knox of Direct Connection, an ISP with around 40,000 subscribers, makes the point succinctly:

> We just couldn't do it [offer the service free] and continue to provide the same level of service. There will always be free connections out there – or rather they will look like free connections. But you pay for it in other ways. (Wapshott, 2000)

The most notable example of not being able to deliver is the ISP AltaVista. Having been highly successful in the US it then decided to offer unmetered access to the Internet, having built up just 1,500 subscribers to its metered service in the UK. In March 2000 it launched its unmetered service and attracted 270,000 potential customers. By August 2000 it realised its systems could not cope with the demand. It had got its figures wrong on being able to fund the service. The offer was withdrawn, resulting in the resignation of the UK managing director.

Another ISP having trouble keeping its promises during 2000 was Freeserve. It offered unlimited access to the Internet for a flat fee of £10 but struggled to cope with the demand. Some customers found that they could not get online when they wanted to and had to resort to the standard pay-as-you-go service. Later that year Freeserve was forced to bar some 700 of its heaviest users (customers who spent more than 16 hours a day online) to make access easier for other subscribers.

Problems with offering free access are not confined to the highly competitive UK market. UOL (Universo Online) which serves the Latin American market withdrew its loss-making Internet access subsidiary, NetGratuita, largely because of its free access policy. It assumed it could cover its administration costs from any resulting e-commerce generated. But only 1 per cent of advertising revenue in Brazil, for example, found its way on to the Internet in 2000. E-commerce revenues in total were less than $300 million despite having 414,921 average visitors per day to UOL.

Such teething problems are clearly irritating for consumers but could be potentially devastating for an e-business hoping to break into the market and create some loyal e-customers. It probably makes sense for an e-business to use a subscriber service, if only to ensure customers can reach you rather than have them log off and have to return some time later – if at all.

Ready to go?

You've heard the hype. You've got the equipment. But do you have the right idea? What seems like a sure-fire winner to you may not be attractive to the market. You could be jeopardising your entire tradi-tional business by over-stretching yourself on what may turn out to be an expensive red herring.

Tales about lastminute.com still abound but there's no denying the facts about sales. By the middle of 2000 the company had managed to build a database of over 700,000 enquirers only to discover that just 15,000 actually bought anything. It will be 2004 before it makes a profit – and that assumes that all will go according to plan.

Clickmango was set up to provide natural health products on the Internet with some high level publicity from one of the investors, actress Joanna Lumley. But by August 2000 it was only making £5,000 of sales a month. It needed to turnover £50,000 a month just to break even. The financiers closed the business in early September 2000, having spent £3 million on marketing.

Letsbuyit.com, the online discount retailer, went to the financial markets to raise cash for what is essentially a good idea – offering discounted goods on the basis of how many customers want to buy at any one time. However, despite a substantial increase in revenues and a leap in gross margins from 2.9 per cent to 9.8 per cent, its annual losses for 2000 increased by 79 per cent. Investors were not impressed. Job losses of 20 per cent of its workforce were announced just to keep the business on an even keel.

What you need to do before you open your doors to the world of cyber customers is to consider very carefully whether your idea fits the model of one which is likely to succeed or is doomed to failure from the very start.

E-business action plan	Useful cyber links
Choose the right equipment	www.dell.com
Think through your domain name	www.nominet.net
Decide which ISP to use (or have your own server)	www.btconnect.com

3   *Will your idea work as an e-business?*

You could be forgiven for thinking that dreaming up an e-business idea that will make you millions takes just a few minutes. Some ideas certainly have that characteristic. But the truth is that such business ideas often die young because no one has thought through the logistical implications of how to deliver the idea at a sensible price. Others fail because they cannot attract enough serious investment funding. Although some recent e-business failures have been highly expensive and heavily publicised, successful concepts that are still in business tend to get less publicity. Often such business failures were due to lack of management control and financial information rather than the concept itself. But is it all hit and miss or are there some trends emerging as to what might survive as an e-business and what will probably fail?

There seem to be several categories for, at the very least, staying in business as an e-business; these are companies that:

- rely on gathering/distributing information;
- need to communicate quickly with the customer;
- act as brokers;
- fulfil a niche market;
- can supply a simple product or service more cheaply online;
- create a new product because of some feature of the Internet.

These are not the only categories – new e-business ideas are being generated every day around the world. But they do not all have to be earth shattering. Underpinning the growth of e-business is the more gradual idea of simply using part of the new technology to improve an established business process. Often this is in the sales area, where the Internet acts as a new channel of distribution, or it is in supply procurement. But Web site know-how also has many applications for all the communication processes within an organisation and beyond it in the distribution of the product or service. You do not have to become a totally virtual business to be a successful e-preneur. You take what you need on a gradual basis, as long as the new way of doing things is more efficient than the old way.

Business examples

Here are just some examples of e-business thinking taken from Business Link case studies... and not all of them are new businesses, by any means.

Fleet Search & Selection

Hugo Hunt is a director of a recruitment agency, Fleet Search & Selection, which covers accountancy, IT and banking.

> We decided about 18 months ago that we wanted a Web site. Recruitment as an industry is moving on to the Net simply because it is a faster and easier way of sending information and searching databases. We had an extra reason in that we were moving into the IT industry where most people are already on the Web. Our site's been more effective than we were expecting. Our IT division now finds between 50 and 55 per cent of candidates through our site and although the figure for clients and jobs is just 5 per cent, even that's growing. Importantly the clients and candidates we find through our site are new. In banking and accountancy the Web site has not proved to be fantastic but it's early days yet. The site's main objective was to attract more candidates and in that it has been well worth the effort and cost.

For Hugo Hunt there was a clear reason for using the new technology. In short, the company wanted more candidates to add to its database and a faster way for information to be exchanged. A Web site was seen to be the way to achieve this business goal. In its initial trials it discovered that that it could have a system feature that would automatically match candidates to vacancies and send them a standard e-mail to gauge their interest. It has yet to use this facility fully as it still worries about being too automated. But there is no doubt that the administrative time this feature saves could in the future be used to provide more resources for interviewing, networking and negotiating.

Sears Parts Direct

Many Internet businesses are based on the principle that if you can provide a simple way for customers to find a complicated product, they will buy that product from you and keep coming back. On a global scale the Sears Parts Direct Web site is a perfect example. The site offers customers a choice of 4 million spare parts for domestic appliances from over 400 manufacturers around the world. A model number search engine does the work. The site also includes a number of helpful tips to assist the customer who may not be a specialist. There are over 40,000 detailed diagrams, a freephone number, a help-line, online ordering and payment systems and a way to track your order so you can see things are happening and, more crucially, find out when it will be delivered.

Teleflorist

Another category for a successful online business is to some extent the opposite of Sears. Customers know exactly what they want but they do not have the time to go to a shop to buy it or take it to the recipient. Flowers are a good example. Teleflorist is the second biggest flower delivery service in the UK after Interflora. Although it only employs about 50 people directly it is the hub of a large organisation with over 2,500 member florists to whom orders are relayed. It can also offer a global service through its overseas affiliates. In the days before the Internet, the system was based on faxes and telephones.

Matt Hampshire, marketing manager, explained what happened as they became an e-business:

Internally we had nobody whose job it was to look at the Internet. But as marketing manager I was becoming increasingly aware of the amount of business going through the Web in other industries. With the help of a Web marketing agency we set up with them as partners in an online flowers ordering business that ran alongside Teleflorist. We shared commission on any sales. They did the software and we handled the orders. In the first year I reckon 10 per cent of all Mother's Day orders – one of our biggest promotions in the year – came directly from the Web site. We also found that average sales values were higher online than through the traditional channels. It may be that people who buy online tend to be wealthier and have less time to shop. They also tend to be men who always spend more than women on flower products in any case.

Widelearning.com

Other e-businesses are built on their cost savings. Widelearning.com provides financial education to both businesses and consumers and is a good example of how the traditional training industry has shifted in a dramatic way towards using the new technology to great advantage. Courses that used to be offered in hotels and through distance learning packages are now offered online. The costs per course have fallen dramatically and standard fees are now only 10 per cent of what they were when they were conducted in a classroom setting. The company has over 100 corporate customers and is currently developing online exams for its financial customers, which can be sat at home on a modular basis. Its investment backers described the service as a 'perfect' online business because it delivers an intangible product more cheaply than it could offline and the target market is 'time poor' and wealthy.

Smaller businesses

The Internet does not necessarily demand you be a large company. In fact it is often said that sole proprietors and partnerships are now able to compete on a global basis for business simply because the cost of distribution by the Web is so low in comparison with traditional marketing methods.

One example is designer Candida Percival. Her company, intofashion.com, sells designer clothes and accessories to a worldwide clientele, all from a one-bedroom flat in London. She buys from both new and established designers but looks for items that have a subtle difference to the norm or that are not available in the high street. She launched her Web site in November 1999 and is expecting to receive a valuation for the potential of her business of around £15 million because of the niche market it services on a global basis.

Another example is Bristol Sweet Mart. It supplies specialist food and spices to local Indian restaurants and started its life with an investment of £50 by a family of refugees from Uganda. It sells only 10 per cent of its lines online but there is a national niche market for exotic food which only the Internet can deliver cost-effectively. It uses a local Web design agency to maintain the site, which also markets what it has to offer through the various search engines. Orders are received by e-mail and fulfilment involves a short walk to the local post office. Payment is with order by credit card.

Health-related organisations

Thirty per cent of all 'hits' on the Internet are said to involve health-related issues. There are now well over 100,000 health sites on the Net. If you want to know about breast cancer for example, you will be put in contact with over 350,000 pages of information using one of the better search engines.

The National Health Service has its own site (www.nhsdirect. nhs.uk) with a nurse-led help-line available on a national basis. The site includes simple advice about a range of conditions, which can lead to self-diagnosis or to getting expert advice via call centres. There is a monthly health feature to tackle specific issues at certain times of the year, such as travelling abroad or what to do in severe weather conditions.

The commercial side of healthcare is booming and in many instances this is due to what the Internet can deliver. Net Doctor (netdoctor.co.uk) offers advice on ailments and only just stops short of offering individual diagnosis and treatment. It provides many self-test procedures to check for such propensities as diabetes or alcoholism. There is also a daily summary of health stories that appear in newspapers and magazines, which you can access overnight.

Pharmacies are well represented as part of this growth in health-related Web sites. They combine the two main reasons for setting up any online business: timely information and convenient distribution. Just one example is Pharmacy2u.co.uk. Registered with the Royal Pharmaceutical Society, the site provides everything you might expect in your local chemist. A clever feature of the online service is that every order is still checked by one of the site's pharmacists before it is dispatched, and pharmacists are available via e-mail if you have any queries. More than 10,000 products are offered across five categories, with free UK delivery for private prescriptions that cost over £30.

Clearly any online business related to health is strictly monitored and you need to be aware of the legal as well as the professional constraints before setting up any health-related Web site.

Go for what already works

Even if you have an existing business there is no rule that says you have to stay within your current boundaries. You may want to branch out into new areas with the new technology and do something completely different. But just to give yourself a fighting chance it may be useful to consider what types of business are generally reckoned to be good e-business opportunities.

On 2 July 2000 *The Sunday Times*, in association with the Bathwick Group, assessed the top hundred e-businesses in Europe, but not purely by sales. Europe's busiest sites were analysed with reference to the criteria shown in Table 3.1. (Visit www.bathwick.com/ir/eleague for more details.)

The scores are to some extent subjective, but the rank order that results from using these criteria provides a good indication of the type of business that is likely to succeed in a virtual environment. The top 10 are shown in Table 3.2.

Table 3.1 E-businesses scoring mechanism

Criteria		Maximum score
*	Management	50
*	Vision	50
*	Technology	20
*	Traffic	20
*	Market reach	15
*	Marketing	15
*	Staff/culture	10
*	Supplier links	10
*	Data management	10
	Total	200

Table 3.2 Top 10 European Web sites

Web site	Score	Sector
1. Sportal.com	164	Sports
2. boxman.com	160	Music/video
3. mondux.com	158	Purchasing
4. netdoktor.com	157	Health
5. peoplesound.com	157	Music
6. beenz.com	156	Loyalty
7. moreover.com	155	News
8. epo.com	154	Finance
9. silicon.com	153	IT news
10. letsbuyit.com	152	Buying club

Looking at these ranked sites, some popular categories emerge. Entertainment, health, news/up-to-date information and purchasing seem to be sectors that have had the most immediate success to date. But not every idea is foolproof. Since this table was compiled, Boxman has gone into receivership. However, if you were to analyse the rest of the top 100 by market sector popularity (see Table 3.3), some patterns are evident.

Table 3.3   Market sector popularity

Most popular sectors	Percentage in top 100
Consumer retail	11
Health	7
B2B supplies	7
Travel services	7
Music/video	6

This is not to say that e-businesses in other sectors will not succeed, far from it. But it does indicate the level of readiness on the part of the consumer and other businesses to trade with such e-businesses on the Internet. Personal services such as the legal profession are probably the least likely to offer serious advice virtually, although even the Law Society does have a Web site (solicitorsonline.co.uk). This is not to say that certain elements of their business would not benefit from a proper, interactive Web-based service. Timely advice about recent legal cases on a worldwide basis is just one example, and uncontested divorces may be another.

   Good Web ideas are not just about business to consumer (B2C). Often the best ones are business to business (B2B) applications where speed of information or distribution efficiency is the key factor (see Chapter 9, B2B – creating new marketplaces).

Would investors back your idea?

Another way to approach the assessment of whether your e-business idea is likely to work is to measure its features against the criteria investors use. Although we are all aware that a dot.com business is still a very young concept and no one has the monopoly on predicting the future, it is worth knowing what professional financial backers look for in a dot.com start-up scenario.

The two questions they will ask first are invariably: 'What is the unique selling point of the business?' and, 'How can this feature be protected against existing and new competition in the marketplace?'

Normally an investment house or a bank to which you might go for funding, if funding is required, will set out a three-stage market analysis for your idea:

1. The first stage would be to assess the growth of your industry and its potential size. If you intend to sell model railway parts to collectors and enthusiasts you could argue that growth may be steady or even declining but that the market is global and therefore there is a good opportunity for a small enterprise to build a satisfying business on a relatively modest scale.

2. The second stage would be to use a market forces model such as Porter's Five Forces, which covers competitive rivalry between existing suppliers, the threat of new entrants, the threat of substitute products, the bargaining power of suppliers and those of buyers. In our model railway parts example, it could be that there are considerable threats from look-alike sites once you go online, but the quicker you build your customer database the more likely you will achieve competitive buying power from your essential suppliers and thereby retain your customers.

3. The third stage is a SWOT (strengths, weaknesses, opportunities, threats) analysis to highlight the key issues for the new e-business. For model railway enthusiasts speed of service may be much less important than acquiring exactly the right part, so close links with suppliers would be of paramount importance and next-day courier services less so.

Guessing for the future

In his book, *Enterprise.com* (1999), Jeff Papows, president and CEO of Lotus Development Corporation, suggests there are at least 'seven areas of industry transformation' that the development of the Internet as a business tool is helping to promote. Some of these could also be a guide for anyone thinking about whether their e-business idea is a sensible one that will pay dividends in the medium or long term as a business investment.

The first one is the practicality of online ordering ('online delivery of products and services'). There are many traditional industries delivering personal products and services that can now be provided by the Internet straight into the home, such as banking, news, entertainment, books and some types of insurance.

The second is 'industry convergence'. When an entire industry adopts a new standard or shares the same technological platform (Windows, for example) this has major implications for me-too products and services. You either conform or you die.

'Value chain extraction' comes next. This means that ways of improving business processes could apply across several industries. Book companies could advise customers on travel options if they knew enough about their lifestyle from their regular book purchases. Banks could offer home billing for utility companies as an independent commercial resource. Does your company undertake any process as part of your business offer that could be adapted to suit another market?   Another idea from Jeff Papows is the way that geography or the physical location of your business is no longer an issue if you are an e-business. If your business charges for professional advice of any description, the Internet provides the way to make this service available on a worldwide basis, subject to language issues.

Some don'ts

In all the euphoria of this brave new e-world it is tempting to rush out and buy all the latest equipment, get a Web site up and running in a week, embark on a massive direct mail campaign to drive people to your new site and wait for the cash to roll in. Like any normal business that is unlikely to happen. As usual, planning is an important discipline. But don't over-plan:

- Don't spend so long getting the technical side right that you miss the market opportunity. If you had waited to start your current business until you knew everything you know now, you would never have got started.
- Don't attempt to be able to offer everyone all the bells and whistles from day one. A gradual approach to costs and services not only gives you time to get things working properly but also helps to retain those early, precious, loyal e-customers for the future.
- Don't just put the product brochure on a screen. It may show you are willing to embrace the new technology but you would only be paying lip service to e-commerce. Any 'brochure ware' needs proper e-commerce back-office systems to make it work and deliver extra profits.
- Don't imagine your entire business will become virtual overnight. It may take years and in some cases only a certain percentage of your current business will ever be conducted over the Internet, depending on what you do.
- Don't assume that a Web site alone means you are an e-trader. There are many examples of successful organisations that use Internet technology for data transfer but which have no Web site at all.

For more don'ts and a few dos, log onto a guide produced by Ernst & Young (www.ey.com/uk) which is part of its e-business reports programme.

Summary

Using the examples above of successful e-businesses, you should now be able to consider your own business or business idea to see if it fits any of these models for success.

At the low-risk end is perhaps some single part of your current business process which might be more efficient, ie cheaper to run, if it were done online. Sales are clearly one area, but so is procurement (buying in supplies).

At the high-risk end, do you have a genuine business concept in a specific niche market that could work if it were virtual? Are there any current competitors? An example could be emergency electricians for vital services such as hospitals, airports or hotels, available nationally without the costs of a service contract.

The normal pattern for most organisations is for one or two processes to be put online initially. Then some months later the online department becomes a separate company or division because its need for resources and its way of doing business are so different from the main business. The third stage is for that separated division to 'invent' a new service or process that has little or no relationship to the original business. It then becomes a distinct, 'new' business with a new corporate structure.

So, assuming you have an idea that has the potential to deliver better profits either for your existing business or as a new business, you have to get the idea up and running in a visual format. In e-business that normally means you need a Web site.

E-business action plan	Useful cyber links
Does your idea fit the Internet model?	www.bathwick.com/ir/eleague
Can the job be done better online?	www.sportal.com
Choose a suitable ISP	www.ispa.org.uk
Plan to procure as well as sell	www.mondus.co.uk

4 *Setting up your Web site*

Your e-business will have no sales people or shop for customers to visit. The only way customers can buy from you is through your electronic Web site. It follows then that the design of your Web site is of vital importance if you are going to be successful. But what are the principles of an efficient Web site?

It may be easier to start by examining what does not go down well with potential customers or visitors to your site. Here are just some examples of criticisms that are often made about poorly designed sites:

'I cannot find the company mentioned in the advertisement on the World Wide Web.'
'The homepage looks like a ghost town.'
'This site looks just like a sales brochure.'
'Links never lead anywhere.'
'This site has very little content.'
'There are so many links I never seem to get into the company's own site.'
'I never get any response to queries.'
'The site doesn't seem to match the company's general marketing.'

Because the Web is open to anyone, both amateur and professional, there are now over 5 million Web sites on the World Wide Web, most of which were designed for personal satisfaction rather than corporate gain. A recent survey by accountants Deloitte & Touche, 'E-business:

Challenges and Opportunities for Growth Companies' (Deloitte & Touche, 2000), assessed the content of Web sites of companies with turnover between £3 million and £10 million. The results are shown in Figure 4.1.

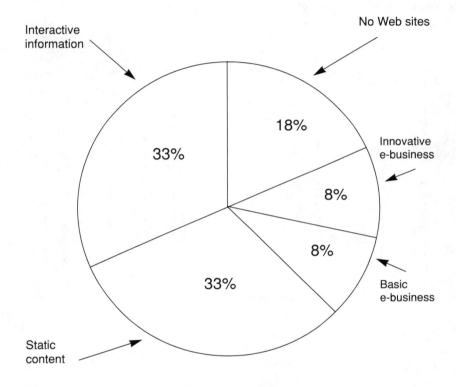

Figure 4.1   Description of companies' Web sites

From this diagram you can see that even amongst relatively established companies there is still a significant proportion, some 18 per cent, with no Web site at all. A third had a passive site with static content, which means they simply put their sales brochure or corporate information there with no opportunity for visitors to interact or contact the company; another third did include such interactive links. But only 16 per cent had been designed as bona fide e-business sites that actively solicited sales or orders.

When the same sample was questioned about what makes a good Web site for business users, they identified a number of main issues, which are shown in Figure 4.2.

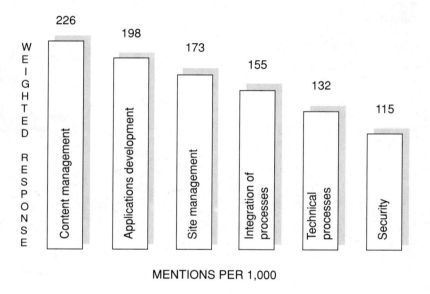

MENTIONS PER 1,000

Figure 4.2 Main issues for business users

The most valued element of Web sites for business users was timely management of the content. To create an effective Web site that people will use repeatedly, the information needs to be updated on a regular basis so it can be relied upon. In some industries this could mean every day or even constantly, such as in financial trading or retail travel. Interestingly, security is listed as an important but not a critical issue.

Go it alone or get some help

As usual in business, there is a price to pay for good advice. When you set about developing a site you can either go to a Web designer to build a bespoke site or use one of the many online companies offering Web site design via the screen, such as NTLShopbuilder or Shopcreator. Which one you choose depends on the complexity of what you are trying to achieve. If you are a retailer for example, and have a pretty good idea that you simply want to put your products online for customers to buy, then creating your store online is relatively straight-forward.

Shopcreator.com is just one of many companies that claim they can create your retail business online within a few hours. The instructions are simple enough for even first-time users to follow, but the features are comprehensive enough for larger companies to use too. Shopcreator's advice is to start with just a few product lines first to gauge response.

The features Shopcreator offers include:

- receiving orders and payments online;
- creating a corporate design;
- adding personalised text;
- registration with search engines;
- stock control;
- digital security for payments;
- e-mail response collection;
- unlimited number of products featured;
- managed on a 24-hour basis;
- links to other sites.

There are a number of versions depending on your budget and what you want to include on your site. The costing structure is based on an initial design fee of a few hundred pounds with monthly hosting and service fees. This second charge depends on the number of products you want to feature, which could range from 50 to 100,000. Shopcreator's homepage is shown in Figure 4.3.

Figure 4.3   Shopcreator's homepage

Elements of effective Web site design

Web site design is often a matter of personal taste. For many small businesses, buying design online is perfectly adequate for getting started, but as the business grows and you learn more about the dynamics of how electronic buyers buy and the importance of marketing your site, some design principles emerge that will improve the effectiveness of your investment.

Ease of navigation

When you 'surf' the Net you will come across a large number of sites that look cluttered and complex to use. The process of investigating a site for what it can offer is known as 'navigation'. It is the designer's job to make your site easy to navigate.

The first issue to confront is all the different groups of visitors your site may attract; they will not all be potential buyers. Depending on your product you may have visitors from the press, students, job-seekers, market researchers and overseas surfers. Your design should include clear signposts for such non-buying visitors to follow and a way for them to return to your homepage with the minimum of back-clicking.

If they are potential buyers you will need to consider the various categories they may fall into. They could be simply searching for up-to-date prices or information, or they may want to express a desire to purchase at some future date (lead generation). They may want someone to call them to discuss a particular item, or they may be looking for a certain type of product.

Keeping track of what they have spent so far on their visit may be important as they may have a specific budget. Easy access to the order form will be appreciated for those in a hurry. A map may be useful for those who simply want to know how to visit your premises as well as a full address and telephone number.

The Early Learning Centre is a good example of a Web site that makes it easy for customers to both search for suitable purchases and to buy online. It even has a gift-finder feature that can list products suitable as gifts for children by age and interest category. Its homepage is shown in Figure 4.4.

The golden rule of good site navigation is for visitors to be able to find what they want within three clicks. If they cannot you may need to redesign the 'architecture' of the site to make it simpler for site visitors.

Simple homepage design

The first image your e-customers will see when they visit your Web site will be your homepage. It makes sense therefore to spend some considerable time thinking about how it looks and what to put on it. At

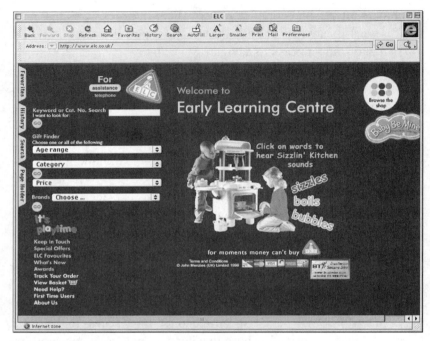

Figure 4.4 Early Learning Centre homepage

the outset you will need to consider what you want visitors to do. Some of the examples mentioned above are full service e-commerce sites in that they are designed to handle the full retail transaction, from interest to purchase and eventual delivery. But not all e-businesses need to be like this. The key issue is to feel comfortable with your use of the new technology at all stages.

If you simply want to tell potential customers that you exist, with the aim of attracting them into your retail premises, the design of your Web site should be subordinated to that overall aim. Your homepage could feature a picture of your retail site or even a picture of you to give it the personal touch. The site would include a visual list of products, your address and contact details, a map and perhaps some information of general interest that can be updated in order to attract visitors to return on a regular basis. Special prices or seasonal product offers are examples. If you are running any kind of sales promotion in the retail outlet, you could feature it on your site with a time deadline to encourage people to visit your store.

If your site is really to gather leads for you to follow up, your homepage should include a way for potential customers to register their details with one click rather than have them visit the whole site before they can express their interest. Such sites need to include lots of reassurance that the enquirer is doing the right thing, so it's a good idea to include some testimonials from existing customers on the homepage. Another feature of lead generation sites is the facility for the visitor to ask questions, so an FAQ (frequently asked questions) link on the homepage is essential, as is an e-mail response facility. It is likely that visitors to your site will already be psychologically ready to buy, so always include a contact telephone number on the homepage.

The third type of site is one with full e-commerce facilities. The homepage needs to be particularly well thought through, as once people leave the site they may never come back. The homepage needs to sell, so do not be shy about how to buy or how to contact your company by telephone or e-mail. As you do not know in advance what type of visitor you are going to attract you will need to provide category or market feature icons so that specific types of visitor can click straight through to what they want to buy. Because of the need to constantly reassure people that buying on the Web is safe, you should always include reference to your secure payment accreditation on the homepage. Verisign.com, for example, provides the Verilink accreditation system; see Figure 4.5.'

Whichever type of e-business you want to operate, the style of the homepage should reflect your likely customers in tone and texture. A site aimed at war veterans may need to be very simple and uncluttered, bearing in mind the likely age and technical ability of the potential visitors. But a site for motor-racing enthusiasts, mostly male and young, could be very 'busy', including lots of links to other sites and with a scroll format rather than a fixed, screen-sized page format so that you can fit more into the homepage.

Figure 4.5 Verilink accreditation system

Simple architecture

Web site architecture describes the route a visitor to your site may take once he or she leaves the homepage. Because your aim is to enable your visitors to reach the information they want as quickly as possible you need to design their 'journey' carefully. If you are a retailer you may want to encourage visitors to explore your site in a particular way so that they do not miss your latest bargains.

Figure 4.6 is a diagram of a typical plan for a Web site. As you can see there are several options after the homepage, depending on the type of visitor expected. Other sites are organised by product category or the service required, but the more effective sites begin with customer types.

Once your visitors confirm their interest in a particular category, they may then wish to have more information or move straight to purchase. The design of the Web site needs to provide easy ways for visitors to return to previously visited pages or the homepage, rather than have to retrace their steps, page by page.

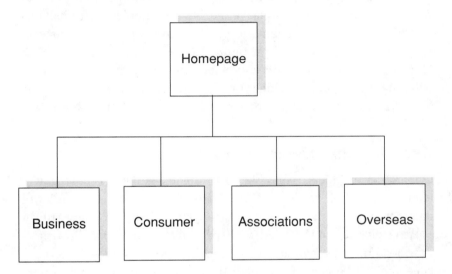

The 'extroverted' Web site reflects your market,
not your product lines

Figure 4.6   Typical Web site architecture

Include links

Another aspect of Web site design is to provide links to related products. A visitor looking for a particular book, for example, may be interested in books in a similar category, so the page should include an electronic link to that section. Similarly, special interest sites may include a link to a completely different Web site of complementary products, owned by another retailer as a kind of added-value service. The Ancestral Instruments site (www.ancestral.co.uk) includes a link to 'Uillean Pipes' within the body of the Web site, because Ancestral Instruments only deals with early bagpipes and mediaeval fiddles. Far from encouraging people to leave the site it reinforces their view that the original site is of genuine use and visitors will return whenever they have a similar query in the future. However, in your enthusiasm to be as helpful as possible do not include too many links, as it can be irritating for visitors waiting to enter other sites and you could lose customers who may not bother to come back to you as a result.

Keep images under control

One of the technical issues yet to be solved is the speed of down-loading data. Colour pictures and video in particular require a lot of data compared with text messages. If you include too many still or moving pictures on any particular page the speed at which visitors download the information may be impaired. Visitors may also experi-ence similar problems with colour backgrounds that cover the entire page area. Not everyone will have the latest machines or the fastest data links on the market. The last thing you want is for your visitors to leave the site early because they become impatient.

Before you commit your site to the Web always test it with a number of types of user to see if there are any problems with the speed of images to be downloaded. One large image will have more impact in printed media, but if visitors have to wait too long for it to appear on their screens, your site will be less successful. At present sites with mostly text are more effective, although this will change as the tech-nology that carries the data gets better.

Careful use of special effects

New software is being released all the time to assist designers to produce Web page graphics. However, what looks good on the designer's Macintosh computer may not translate very well onto the typical visitor's screen. There are many technically excellent software packages currently in use by designers (Dreamweaver, ColdFusion, for instance) to add special features to client Web sites. One example is 'Flash'. Corporate Web site designers often use this package from Macromedia to add life to what would otherwise be fairly dull statements of corporate achievement or general business information. Flash is characterised by flashing animation of boxes, dissolves and moving images. In acknowledgement of the fact that not every visitor is prepared to wait for the site to download or can read flash sites, many sites ask you to choose whether you want to view the site with or without 'flash'. The fact that the site authors have to ask the question suggests perhaps that the feature should not be there in the first place.

Invent a community

It may sound a bit West Coast, USA to suggest you 'invent a community' with your site, but you would be amazed how loyal users can be when they find a site of like-minded visitors. If they are loyal it means they will return to the site again and again just to find out what is going on. For example, if you run a car dealership site you could add regular updates on the position of local road works or offer advice about taking your car abroad. You might even suggest non-motorway routes between popular local towns and allow visitors to add their own favourite routes. All visitors could be encouraged to leave their e-mail address to which you could then send special offers or other relevant product information on the assumption that they are motoring enthusiasts.

You are allowed to be creative

Just because your site may be B2B does not mean you have to be formal and serious. You will have a good idea who your main visitors are. By engaging them in some form of interaction you will encourage them to return to your site rather than that of a competitor, and purchasing loyalty will increase as a result.

A supplier of engineering parts could run a weekly competition on screen, perhaps based on Grand Prix to encourage purchasers to visit the site on a regular basis.

A florist could enable customers to personalise their gift by allowing them not only to choose the type of flower but also the type of card and perhaps also to choose a message from a pre-prepared selection.

An accountant could build a profile of online customers so that future marketing messages could be directed to the relevant group of customers rather than just sending out blanket offers. Clients could be grouped by end of financial year, or their birthday, or by their industry sector so that important but relevant news can be relayed as quickly as possible.

Newspaper publishers are currently experimenting with 'personalised' newspapers that would carry only the type of news topics that you have indicated you want to read. Your daily, personalised edition of *The Times* or whatever would be available online to download each day and be tailored precisely to your particular interests.

There may be a number of other elements you will need to fit in to your design. Directions to the order form and reassuring security icons are important design aspects that need to be on the homepage, whatever else has to be there. For some businesses reciprocal advertising on the homepage may be the only way they can keep their costs for the site within reason. But whatever your particular needs are, you should always consider what response your visitors will have to any proposed design before you agree to add to what is likely to be an already crowded area of available screen.

For very simple designs most of the ISPs provide free software that you can download and with the minimum of experience you will be able to design an adequate site. Microsoft's Internet Explorer has FrontPage Express and Netscape has the Communicator suite of programs. With a digital camera or a scanner you can even add product or service pictures from your current brochure, if there is one, to add interest.

Cost guidelines for Web sites

As you saw from the introductory chapter to this book, the costs of setting up a Web site to do the right job for your particular business can vary depending on its complexity. Table 4.1 shows a typical menu of costs a small business might expect to budget for a simple site. However, a more complex site would be more likely to cost between £6,000 and £10,000.

Table 4.1   The cost of setting up a simple site

Web site items	Cost
Design visuals, style	£1,750
Page production for 10 pages	£800
Visitor response page	£100
Set up, testing	£100
Page storage on server (per annum)	£150
Site maintenance (five hours per annum)	£250
Total	**£3,150**

Developing and servicing the site

According to a survey of Web designers conducted by Hay Management Consultants in 2000, more than a quarter of client organisations had difficulties trying to recruit and retain their own Web designers and developers. At present the market is growing so strongly that people with Web design skills are able to make much more money as freelancers than working for an individual company. Even if you do manage to train up your own staff there is a strong likelihood that they will be poached, sometimes with a substantial bonus, to join an agency within six months, so great is the demand for these skills.

As a small business the best route forward may be to work in tandem with a Web designer initially while building up your own resource to handle routine upgrades or administrative amendments. Most companies make a board director responsible for e-commerce development, but few have specific IT skills. Because of this there is a danger that IT projects are slow to get off the ground and you could end up buying inappropriate software or be building a Web site that does not integrate with your market in the way you expected.

For an e-business to work well, all those involved in its execution, from finance and sales through to distribution and after-sales need to be aware of what is being developed. No single department or board director has all the answers. Contributions need to be taken from right across the business where your new e-customers are going to be interacting with your staff.

An important routine check is to test the site by asking friends and colleagues to use it. You would be surprised how many sites go live with basic spelling mistakes or no clear way to find the order form.

It is always better to build up your own in-house resource as a vital part of your e-business plan otherwise you could find yourself being hostage to any price rises your external resource decides to levy. More importantly, you may never learn the fundamentals of how your site is constructed and have to rely on your supplier even for minor program changes for many years to come.

E-business action plan	Useful cyber links
Learn about good Web site design	www.iwks.com
Ask for expert help	www.ukwebdesigners.net
Take time with your homepage	www.peoplesound.com
Who will service your site?	www.isi.gov.uk

5 Collecting cash and VAT, securely

Unless the total online shopping environment – sites and payment mechanisms – is made more secure, some customers will never have the confidence to explore the opportunities.

Anna Bradley, National Consumer Council

All businesses need to collect customer payments. An e-business is no exception. But a business that generates bad debts is arguably not worth pursuing at all. Lack of confidence in how secure the World Wide Web is has put off many would-be e-preneurs from getting started. This attitude causes problems whether you are a seller trying to market your goods or a buyer wishing to make a purchase. The Love Bug virus, which corrupted hundreds of thousands of computers around the world, was disseminated by a single computer technology student in the Far East.

In July 2000, Powergen, the utility company, had stored the records of over 7,000 customers who pay their bills by direct debit on an Internet file. Unfortunately each customer could view the payment records of all the other direct debit payers with a minimum of technical ability. Powergen had to offer all its customers an incentive of £50 to change their details to avoid this program error and serious lapse of security.

The banking industry is particularly vulnerable to the threat of Internet-related security lapses as bad publicity could easily cause a rush on the withdrawal of funds under management. As banks become increasingly Internet-driven, so does the danger of fraud and lack of security. Statistics compiled by the Wall Street Transcript and Qualistream in 2000 about the existence of online banking around the world revealed that the UK had one of the highest pene-trations, with 30 per cent of all banks having some online capability. Collectively they manage the finances of over 175,000 UK businesses. Only Spain and Germany have a higher percentage of banks offering online payment services. Concern over how to con- vince business customers that online banking is as safe as offline credit clearing has been matched by a number of security initiatives. But the systems will have to be developed at breakneck speed if they are going to meet the demand. In 1998 only 3 per cent of global transactions were under-taken through online systems by the banks. Fletcher Research has esti-mated that by 2005 over three-quarters of 'presentments' will be handled through the Internet.

The basics of business trust

For buyers and sellers to transact online with confidence, they need to be reassured about the five basic trusts when undertaking a transaction electronically:

1. authentication: 'I can prove who I am';
2. integrity: 'If you alter my order, I will know';
3. confidentiality: 'No one else can read my order details and what I paid for it';
4. authorisation: 'I have the authority to transact this order';
5. non-repudiation: 'I cannot go back on my word unless you allow me to'.

Passwords, encryption, identity certificates and digital signatures can satisfy all these needs.

Encryption

To ensure that your customers can give you confidential financial information or indeed any other kind of private data, their information can be encoded in such a way that a specific key is required to decode it. Normally sellers will 'encrypt' their site for customers so that any details of the transaction such as a credit card number or a bank account can only be viewed by the seller. Customers may also create their own transaction passwords before they make an order. This provides an additional level of security.

Following the five principles of business trust outlined above, buyers first need to prove that they are who they say they are before they can successfully transact. If they are paying by credit card the amount is collected automatically in the same way that a retailer would collect payment, so establishing true identity is less important. However, in a business to business scenario the authority to transact needs to be established. This is achieved by the purchaser being given a private key or password to the buying system. This key is used to encrypt any confidential commercial information sent via the Internet. It can also be used to sign transactions at the end of the order. More sophisticated devices such as digital keys on smart cards, voice recognition and even fingerprint scanning are being developed for the future and may one day become commonplace for e-commerce if costs come down.

When dealing with consumers it is important to establish absolute trust between your business and the customer, especially if you intend to sell goods on a global basis. There are a number of Internet trust products you can buy online to add to your Web site. VeriSign is currently the most widely used verification system with its memorable Verilink padlock icon. The service includes a digital certificate that shows that your business is an accredited business and has secure systems, whether you have your own server or use a secure service provider outside the business. Customers can view your certificate online and when they log on to your site they can see the Verilink icon on the home or ordering page.

There are other systems too. Trust UK runs a similar system and was set up by the Department for Trade and Industry, the Consumers Association and the Alliance for Electronic Business. It acknowledges that the business follows an acknowledged privacy code and can provide robust facilities for customer privacy and secure payments.

The Academy of Internet Commerce operates a seal of approval system for businesses that are members and have satisfied the criteria for transparency, security and strong customer service routines. When customers click on their icon the full wording of their service charter and security charter pops up for customers to read.

Whichever system you choose, they all include an accreditation icon that acts as a proof of security and encrypt any confidential information received from the buyer when they buy.

Digital signatures

There has been much debate in recent years about contracting for services online. Some commentators were getting concerned about whether electronic signatures would be acceptable with the advent of e-commerce. However, the pressure to develop an electronic signature system has come mostly from outside the UK, as under UK law the requirement for signatures has only ever applied to certain specific documents. Within the UK a contract can be made verbally or sometimes by implication, depending on the situation. This topic will be dealt with in more detail in Chapter 6. Suffice it to say that electronic signatures are now acceptable by law in the UK as a means of verifying a contractual arrangement. This change in the law is more for the benefit of businesses that trade internationally and is part of the wider move to harmonise business practices across the EU.

Virtual payment systems

Credit card fraud has been a feature of business to consumer transactions since the invention of the credit card. But it is both unfair and inaccurate to think that the problem is somehow worse on the Internet. In fact credit card fraud in e-commerce is remarkably low because of the security devices mentioned above and is inherently no worse than buying retail. The National Consumers League of America estimated that credit card fraud on the Internet in 1999 was just $3.2 million, which is very low when you compare that with the figure of total online transactions over the entire year.

However, the fact that both the buyer and the seller may be unknown to each other has resulted in a number of ways to overcome the issue of whether the customer will pay. Internet or virtual banks now exist where regular online purchasers can store their wealth or at least part of it in cyberspace. Virtual tokens or credits are purchased by the customer, who pays for goods and services online using these credits. That way sellers know they will be paid and customers can keep track of their Internet expenditure. CompuServe runs its own system called CyberCash, which it manages for its own customers to facilitate online purchasing.

There is no doubt that there will be many other ways developed in the future to enable consumers and businesses to make payments in a secure way. But it has to be recognised that at present still by far the most popular way to avoid these issues is for e-businesses to contact potential customers by telephone or fax to discuss a suitable payment method, once an order has been placed. There may be a section of your market that will always want to pay for goods in this way until such time as they have total confidence in the new technology.

Security is not just about payment

For a small business, collecting payments is a crucial issue, especially in the early days when budgets are tight and continuing bad debts could make the whole venture unfeasible. The security devices described above go a long way to making online payments as secure if not more secure than traditional trading, as in most cases payment is received long before the goods are dispatched. But creating a secure Web site means more than just being paid promptly. Because the Internet is based on easy and rapid exchange of information there is always the possibility that people entering your system could do damage while they are there. In some cases this could include your own staff. The opportunity of e-business is also therefore a potential threat. For that reason every e-business should have a sound systems security policy. Your e-business policy review should include the following issues at the very least:

- confidentiality of data;
- access from outside;
- risk assessment;
- partner requirements;
- counter measures;
- trusted application service providers.

The traditional approach in large company IT systems security is to throw a protective cloak around the entire system so that only people within the system can access data and programs. Within this closed universe, access by staff tends to follow a hierarchical pattern based on their need for the data. External users are rarely if ever given access to it. Because e-commerce relies on people and organisations outside the business having direct access to some of your operational systems, you will have to decide on more flexible boundaries.

Customers will need to run some of your internal processes and access certain data, but it is vital that they can only view and change information they are authorised to access. The problem with the perimeter approach is that all system routines are treated with equal importance, relying on the trust factor of users. With 'ubiquitous security' you can be more selective and only allow authorised visitors access to specific parts of your system.

Breaches of security generally fall into three types: operational, financial and legal. On the operational side hackers are probably the biggest danger, but they tend to target larger organisations. The most likely breach of operational security will come from someone within the organisation with a grudge to bear or simply to demonstrate such a breach can be achieved. Loss of electronic information can be a significant issue if there are no back-up files. Financial breaches could be much more serious resulting in corrupt files and, in the worst scenario, fraudulent payments. Legal issues of security include impersonation of trusted users, violation of safety regulations and the theft of copyrighted material. A major technical issue currently being looked at is how to make mobile telephones secure; some experts are predicting a significant risk of fraudulent purchases in the future unless verification systems can be improved within the context of SIM card technology.

For small businesses the cost of developing bespoke security systems for an e-business are likely to be very high. However, there are a number of security products that can be bought off the shelf to manage the security aspects of a new e-business. The expenditure by businesses on so-called TASPs (Trusted Application Service Providers) is predicted to treble in volume over the next three years as demand grows. Ovum, an Internet security specialist (www. ovum.com) reckons that expenditure on system security will balloon to over £35 billion globally by 2005 from a virtual standing start of around £5 billion in 2001.

The message is a simple one. All e-businesses need to be secure, so making your site secure before you start to trade should be an important part of your business plan.

Delivering the goods

At the least complex end of the e-commerce spectrum, the Internet is nothing more than a telephone ordering mechanism. If you have systems to deal with orders by phone, whether you deal with consumers or business to business, there is no reason why your system should change very much. But there are two characteristics of the new technology that may make you rethink your current fulfilment routines: speed and international customers.

Speed of delivery

In the brave new world of the Internet, offering 28 days for delivery from the date of order is not why customers use the World Wide Web. Invariably they are people with little time to shop, or business people in a hurry wanting a fast turnaround. Implicit in the e-business promise is a speed of delivery that encourages the buyer to keep buying online rather than visiting a retail or wholesale outlet.

Early experience in the UK has not been good. Over the 1999 Christmas period estimates from retailers' associations revealed that around 25 per cent of all online goods ordered during the Christmas period were either mis-posted or late. Jungle.com was just one company taken to task by a popular consumers' television programme for being unable to deliver goods in time. They readily admitted they were overwhelmed by the demand.

One way to be able to keep your promises is to organise stock on a 'just in time' (JIT) basis. Close communications will be needed with your suppliers, preferably online, to ensure you do not run out of basic stock and annoy your valuable customers. In an ideal world you should handle the fulfilment yourself in-house to stay in control, especially if you are dealing with perishable goods or have major spikes of demand over peak periods.

A good example of an online business that deals with 'perishable goods' is TheTrainline.com. Launched in October 1999, this joint venture between Virgin Travel and Stagecoach sells rail tickets online, with a monthly turnover of about £10 million, which is about twice as much as the average train operator. The big selling point for its customers is not to have to queue at the ticket office, especially if they are running late. But delivery of the tickets is a vital issue. It guarantees delivery by post the next day, or tickets can be collected at the nearest station.

But quick delivery often means high costs and it is quite possible that you will have customers who would be prepared to wait a day or two longer for a keener price. Many e-businesses offer staggered delivery prices based on how quickly the customer wants the goods dispatched. You will need to consider within your own market how important it is to offer swift delivery and what processes you can put in place to ensure you meet your deadlines. It may well be that by giving the dispatch job to your suppliers or a logistics specialist you will be able to shave a few hours or days off your delivery time and so steal a march on the competition.

Because delivery and logistics are such a vital part of the e-business offering, a number of traditional product delivery companies have transformed themselves by becoming e-fulfilment specialists.

Standard Photographic

Standard Photographic was founded in 1934 to produce photographic film and currently turns over around £25 million. In the 1960s it stopped making film to concentrate on delivering film to retail outlets. By 2000 it had decided that its expertise in delivering film products to over 3,500 customers by 9 am the next day was a skill e-businesses could use. It created a new division of the company called iNet Distribution and expects to achieve revenues of over £1 million during 2001 from its distribution service for e-business customers. It is only 5 per cent of total group business, but it is a start.

Managing customer expectations has become a way of life for many e-businesses. Rather than hope that the customer will not notice any delay, successful e-businesses are managing the communications process by sending confirmatory e-mails when orders are received, informing customers of any delays for specific products, providing e-mail or telephone links on the Web site so that the customer can query delivery times, and building in order-tracking mechanisms so that customers can check for themselves how their order is progressing.

Delivering overseas

Once you publish your Web site you will be visible in around 200 countries worldwide for 24 hours a day. Compared with a traditional business that represents a lot of marketing exposure. Even if only a tiny proportion of net users visit your site it is inevitable that you will receive a number of enquiries from overseas. You may even get some direct orders. You need to be ready.

You could decide that you do not want to take orders from abroad, at least for the first year while you get your e-business under way. But it will be useful to keep a record of 'hits' by country, asking visitors to leave their details for future marketing use.

If your plan is that you would like to take orders from overseas from the beginning, there are a number of issues to resolve:

- translating the site into foreign languages;
- 24-hour access for customers;
- overseas deliveries;
- import and export regulations;
- currencies;
- taxes;
- terms and conditions.

One approach to doing business overseas is to start by only taking orders from English-speaking countries such as the United States, Canada, Australia and New Zealand. That way you avoid the costs of translation and cut your teeth on the actual logistics of overseas deliveries. But sooner or later you will have to respond to the non-English-speaking market even if only to decline to take their money. It is predicted that by 2002 there will be 300 million Internet users of which at least half will not be English-speaking. Fortunately there are a number of software aids to help you.

Some search engines (see Chapter 7) offer free online translation services, which will be perfectly adequate for general, unambiguous communication with foreign customers. You can find the AltaVista translation service on babelfish.altavista.digital.com. A more complex version, such as wordlingo.com, allows you to have longer passages translated for free. If you feel fairly confident that you can handle the translation of simple messages yourself, you may find the online language dictionaries to be a useful addition to your software. Sites such as www.foreignword.com give you access to hundreds of online language dictionaries to help you brush up your vocabulary. However, all translation tasks are a minefield if you are unsure of your ground. Misunderstandings, particularly about the products you are offering and the terms of payment, could prove expensive.

If your business is even slightly technical the only professional solution is to have key pages translated by an accredited translator. The Institute of Translation & Interpretation has a Web site (www.iti.org.uk) where you can find translators who are expert in your own field so that you can get the best possible translation, however obscure you think your products are. Costs vary by the language required and are charged on a per hundred words basis.

Depending on your market you should consider translating your site into French and/or German first, as these represent major European markets. When you are confident that your delivery procedures are working properly, you could try Spanish next as this will ease your entry into the US market as more people actually speak Spanish than English in the United States, believe it or not. Niche markets may require you to provide a translation, such as into Hebrew or Chinese. A Flemish company called iTranslator is offering to translate these and other unusual languages such as Catalan, using a combination of computers and humans to get the highest possible standards. Pages can be sent online for translation and payment made by credit card.

Things to include for international customers

The most important details to make clear when trading with overseas customers are your terms of business. You need to spell out very clearly your prices and what they include. The customer needs to be in no doubt as to how to pay and what duty might apply to the goods you are dispatching. You will want to specify the details of your delivery policy and sound arrangements for the return of any goods if they are not suitable. It goes without saying that for most e-businesses trading internationally you need to get the payment before you dispatch the goods, whatever the circumstances, as the costs of recovery for you will be very high if the customer refuses to pay.

Prices should be in the customer's local currency or in some circumstances you can use US dollars. Having currency calculators as part of the Web site design for your site is a useful service so that overseas customers can check the costs in their local currency before they decide to buy. One example is www.oanda.com, which can become an integral part of your site, but there are several others that offer various levels of sophistication.

Measurements and weights are often a deciding factor when customers are buying direct, so remember to include such detail both in metric and imperial formats. This information may also have a bearing on your delivery costs, so it is vital to get it right before you commit yourself to delivering on a global basis.

Creating order forms is not the kind of business task every entrepreneur relishes. But for an e-business it is essential to think it through carefully as there will be no sale unless the order form collects all the data you need to complete the order. You can always fax or ring customers to check specific queries, but time zones and the issue of language, not to mention the cost of telephone calls, make this contact route a last resort. In particular, recording addresses with relevant postal codes needs to be reflected in your order form design as such codes can act as a failsafe if the actual address has been wrongly transcribed. You will also need to consider what details you will need from the purchaser to levy VAT if it is relevant (see below).

Selling on the Internet is often a question of building trust. One feature you will find on most professional Web sites is the inclusion of how customers can contact you, either by instant e-mail or by other means. You should always tell customers what time zone you are in so they can call you during your local business hours. If you think you will get a large number of orders from the United States you may need to reorganise your staff so that they are contactable during the evening in the UK, as for most US customers this time period will be their working day.

If you are selling business to business you may have only a handful of overseas customers. In that case it should be simple to obtain trade references through the usual channels, but bear in mind that most directories are out of date by at least a year, sometimes longer, so you need to satisfy yourself that the company can pay before you start dispatching goods abroad unless you intend to take payment first as a trading condition.

Whether you are dealing with consumers or businesses you should always make it as easy as possible for purchasers to pay you. Put your bank details on every order form however small, as there is more chance of tracing the payment if the right coding is attached. The DTI has a useful site for exporters who want to clarify how to trade internationally on the Net. Their 'cyberpark' is www.tradeuk.com.

Terms and conditions

One of the great virtues of being an e-business is that you can control to whom you sell and at what price. No goods need to leave your premises unless you are satisfied with the deal you are making. When you are selling overseas, terms and conditions dictate the type of business you will attract so you need to consider carefully what restrictions if any you might want to place on the acceptance of orders from overseas. Your terms could include receipt of funds before dispatch, a digital signature, or other secure means to establish authority to purchase if it is a business, what they should do about returns or complaints, which currency to pay in, average delivery times depending on location, and which credit cards you will accept. This is by no means an exhaustive list and much will depend on the nature of your business. All terms should be subject to English law if you are trading from England and you should state this in your terms and conditions to avoid any misunderstandings if there is a dispute.

VAT and e-commerce

Value Added Tax poses a number of issues for e-businesses in the UK, many of which are still being debated. It is true to say that EC legislators and tax-raisers have been caught out by the speed of growth of e-commerce and are only just getting to grips with the implications of trading on a global scale from your own back bedroom. For large companies the rules about VAT have not changed and they will know already how to deal with international orders, whether orders come online or offline.

The Internet has created a number of new ways to sell products and services, not only within the local economy but also on a global scale. In brief, this new channel of distribution has a number of new situations for the tax authorities:

- the sale of digitised products, such as computer files, written documents, music and video;
- the sale of physical products that can be ordered over the Net but then delivered through the post;
- the sale of services such as financial and stock market information.

The new distribution channel does not make it easy for the regulatory authorities to collect revenue due from sales. If the costs of items are significantly lower than through traditional channels, this could change the balance of tax contributions and lead one day to a two-tier purchase tax system where VAT on non-electronic commerce sales would have to be increased to compensate for the loss of revenue from e-commerce.

The other approach could be to tax e-commerce even more to cover the costs of collection, particularly with 'virtual' products that cannot be seen or stock-checked. For someone hoping to expand into Internet-related sales it is important to realise that these issues will be debated intensely over the next few years and no one can give guarantees that the regime will not change.

The other new issue facing the tax authorities is the large number of small-scale, inexperienced traders who may not even be registered for VAT and may have only a vague understanding of what the law says. As a budding e-business the last thing you want is a time-consuming VAT investigation in a year's time just as your business is taking off. So, here are the principles as they stand at the moment, but do seek professional advice from your accountant as the rules can be easily misunderstood by the lay person and may well change in the future as e-commerce grows and becomes more complex.

The story of VAT and the Internet started in October 1998 at the OECD (Organisation for Economic Cooperation and Development) Conference in Ottawa. The major trading nations of the Western world decided that they should investigate whether trading on the Internet would be a threat to the identification and collection of VAT. In general they concluded that it would not be. If any action were to be taken at all they should simply try to harmonise VAT principles at any future opportunity to do so. They found that all their members operated purchase taxes such as VAT in broadly the same way although the amounts differed, and therefore there was no need to make sweeping changes just because of the rise of e-commerce. They determined that as a principle VAT should be due in the country of supply, that digitised products should be treated as services, that business to business supplies across borders could be accounted for by 'reverse charge' and that there would be no new taxes.

However, not every country is a signatory to the OECD initiative. Trading history has shown that there would be a big advantage for certain countries with no real resources of their own to set themselves up as a tax-free state when it comes to e-commerce, in the same way that offshore products are sold within the financial services sector.

In November 1999 the UK government followed suit by publishing a report called 'Electronic Commerce'. In it they state their current view: 'Being comprehensive in its nature, VAT is sufficiently robust to capture the majority of e-commerce transactions in its existing form.' In fact, most of the VAT rules for Internet trading are already enshrined in the 1994 VAT Act under Schedule 5, which covers telecommunication services.

However, there are a number of small traders who now only do business on the Internet and somewhat larger traders who are now trading internationally where the rules can get complicated. Here we will take a brief look at VAT with regard to e-commerce and a small business starting up, so that you are aware at the very least of your likely liability if the e-business channel of distribution pushes you into the realms of VAT registration.

E-business with private individuals

There has been some discussion as to whether the whole system could be turned upside down to make consumers keep track of any VAT they pay within the EU. This would have the result of avoiding any discrepancy between e-commerce and traditional purchases. Distortion between domestic and overseas shopping would also disappear so as everyone would be paying the same VAT amount. However, this is unlikely to happen at least in the short term simply because there are too many consumers to collect tax from. The implications for software to track which products should attract VAT and which should not, and the inevitable verification that goods downloaded electronically were being charged at the right price and not being fraudulently lowered to reduce a tax liability, are obvious problems. For the moment no action has been taken and EU governments are keeping a watching brief.

So, what should you expect to charge VAT on if you were to start e-trading tomorrow? Just like any other business in the UK, if you are selling goods to UK consumers you will need to charge VAT at the prevailing rate, currently 17.5 per cent, provided you have reached the minimum threshold of turnover to be registered as a collector of VAT. This is currently £52,000. If you are selling goods to a country within the EU you will need to charge the UK rate of VAT on goods sold to individuals within that country. If your turnover in any EU country exceeds their local limit (anywhere between €25,000 and €71,000 depending on the country in question), you will need to register for VAT in those member states. Subsequent sales will therefore be liable to VAT in the UK or in the country of destination depending on whether you are registered, although goods worth less than €22 will not be liable to VAT at all.

If your customers are outside the EU then you do not need to charge VAT. It is possible to avoid having to register for VAT in the member states by initially exporting the goods to a place outside the EU and then having them sent on to your customers. However, this is both costly and takes time, which is not usually why your customers would buy from you as an e-business in the first place.

Customs duty may also be payable on some deliveries both within and outside the EU, so it is important to know what the charges will be so that you can invoice the customer accordingly before you dispatch the goods.

The sale of digitised services in which the 'goods' are downloaded in electronic format (books, videos, etc) rather than being delivered in a physical format can cause some anomalies as to whether they attract VAT or not. For example, sheet music sold as a printed piece of paper under current rules in the UK would not attract VAT, but it would if it were to be downloaded in digital form by a UK customer from a UK Web site. If in doubt, ask for some professional help.

E-business with commercial concerns

Business to business transactions within the UK attract VAT in the normal way, provided you are trading above the current threshold limits. Transactions outside the UK are not subject to VAT but you will need to keep proof of export for each item sent abroad. If the corporate buyer is within the EU no VAT is payable provided the recipient's EU VAT number is shown on sales documentation and evidence is retained to prove the goods left the UK.

To be able to keep records of this information your Web site should include sufficient screen space to capture it so that you can provide the right level of detail when it comes to your end-of-year reporting. You should be able to identify whether the customer was a private individual or a business and how much VAT was levied depending on the circumstances of each sale. It is a good idea to reserve the right to change your prices in your terms and conditions should local rates of VAT change suddenly.

When to charge

Figure 5.1 should help you to decide whether to charge VAT to individual retail customers or what records to keep depending on where your e-customers are likely to be based.

Electronic cash and the future of VAT

Electronic cash is a new form of payment that raises specific questions about any kind of purchase or consumption tax and its collection. Many people already use the electronic chip in a telephone card to pay for phone calls, so the principle of electronic cash or credit being widely used is just a question of retailer software and hardware. 'Cybercash' already exists, but electronic cash currently differs from ordinary cash in its anonymity. People often use cash for reasons of privacy. They also like the convenience of being able to pay for low-value goods and services with the minimum of effort.

One way forward with electronic cash would be to issue the credits already taxed. A £1,000 credit of electronic cash would be debited as £1,175 to account for VAT. The customer would then use this method to pay for goods either on the Internet or in a shop without having to account for VAT. But this is unlikely to be a popular concept for the average consumer.

For most businesses the principles of VAT will not change. But the current reporting requirements mean you will need to think through how you are going to keep accurate records of your e-business

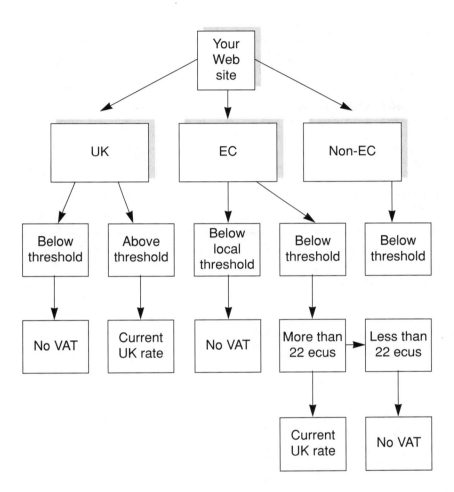

Figure 5.1 VAT decision tree

customers, especially as there will be no paper to file as evidence. Another reason to get it straight from the very beginning is to determine any liability you may have in the event that errors are made. VAT inspectors will be sympathetic up to a point, but at the end of the day their job is to collect tax from you, regardless of whether you have actually collected it from your customers first. So tread carefully.

E-business action plan	Useful cyber links
Research the software for secure payment	www.worldpay.com
Devise a security policy for your business	www.virginbiz.net
Decide on your delivery procedures	www.free-ebd.com
Make sure you collect enough VAT	www.businessadviceonline.org.uk

6 *Legal issues and your e-business*

Just before we dash off to start marketing our new venture it is worth considering if there are any legal problems to be wary of. After all, e-business is a real business just like any other with the possibility of damages and punitive legal action if things go wrong. Large companies take legal issues in their stride and they often identify a budget for legal matters at the beginning of the year. But for a small business one slip could mean not only having to close down the new e-business but perhaps other related businesses of which your e-business is only a part, to pay costs or to make reparation.

Potential legal problems

There are number of identifiable legal issues that have come to light over the past two or three years which are particular to e-commerce. Few have so far been tested in the UK courts, so looking at precedence is not much help if you want to have categorical answers before you decide to do something specific. In many instances the fact that the dispute arose through e-trading proves to be incidental, as current trading law already exists to deal with most problems. But because e-commerce is relatively new it is as well to be aware of areas in the development of your e-business that could give rise to legal issues:

- ● Set up.
- – acquiring a suitable domain name;
- – retrieving an existing domain name;
- – copyright assignment for software;
- – copyright assignment for your Web site design.
- ● Running the Web site.
- – copyright in general;
- – substantiating product claims;
- – data protection;
- – limitations when using links;
- – use of trade marks;
- – trading presence.
- ● Selling online.
- – contracting online;
- – language choice;
- – tax;
- – electronic signatures;
- – payment methods;
- – delivery liability;
- – other countries' laws.

As you can see from this basic list there is a lot to consider, but if you worried about everything that could possibly result in a law suit you would not be in business in the first place. For traders in the EU most of these issues will be dealt with by reference to the EC Directive on Distance Selling, which was designed to protect consumers when they buy goods in a way other than face-to-face, in other words, at a distance. It came into force on 31 October 2000. To this, as a UK business, you will need to add a passing knowledge of the Electronic Communications Act, which came into force in May 2000.

Potential problems when you set up your Web site

Using the fictional company, MK Music Centre, I am most grateful to Gary Assim, partner with Shoosmiths Solicitors in Milton Keynes, for creating these typical e-business start-up scenarios. I have paraphrased his advice after each example.

MK Music Centre: examples of legal issues

A retailer sells musical instruments under the trading name 'MK Music Centre'. It has done so for 20 years and has built up a reputation. It decides to start trading on the Internet and applies to register www.mkmusiccentre.co.uk. That domain has already gone. A search identifies the retailer's main competitor, 'Bedford Music Centre', as the domain owner.

This is a clear case of 'passing off' as the Bedford Music Centre has no reason to own the domain name and is hoping that consumers will be directed to the Web site by search engines, thinking that they have found the MK Music Centre site, their main rivals.

Having successfully obtained its new domain name, MK Music Centre carries out further searches on the Internet and discovers the following already existing Web sites:

www.miltonkeynesmc.co.uk, which sells musical instruments;
www.mkmc.co.uk, which is a motoring club for private members;
www.mkmusiccentre.com, which also sells musical instruments.

The test to see if you would be infringing someone else's trademark is to apply the two questions: is the name identical or similar and is the product or trade sector identical or similar? In the first case above the domain name is similar and the area of trade is identical, so MK Music Centre would be well advised to avoid a possible suit for trade mark infringement.

In the second case although the name is identical the area of trade is not, so MK Music Centre should be able to register mkmc.co.uk as a musical instrument supplier.

In the third case the name is identical as is the area of trade, so it looks at first sight that MK Music Centre cannot use it. However, because the address is a .com address it is by definition hosted out of the USA (as are all .com, .org and .net addresses) and it could be argued that a local company could use it for UK or European sales. In practice MK Music Centre would need to have any dispute decided by ICANN (The Internet Corporation for Assigned Names and Numbers) at www.icann.org and for a fixed fee it will be able to get a decision on the matter which would be binding.

MK Music Centre talks to WDC Web design about producing the design for its new Web site. It verbally agrees that WDC should start work straight away. After a few weeks MKMC starts having problems with WDC about the quality of its work and the deadlines it has missed for completion. MKMC wants to give the rest of the job to another Web design company.

This is an example of breach of contract and should be straightforward to remedy. However, a verbal agreement would not automatically prevent the Web design house from retaining the copyright, which would force MK Music Centre to start all over again with another design company. To prevent this from happening, MK Music Centre should have had an agreement in writing to grant copyright of the design to itself and obtain a readable copy on disk of the design at each stage so that a new company could continue the work in case of dispute.

MK Music Centre has collected a great deal of information about its Web site visitors and customers on its payments page over the past three months of trading. It wants to use this information to send them details of special offers and other services.

MK Music Centre needs to register as a 'data user' in accordance with the provisions of the Data Protection Act (see below). It should have put a notice on its Web site that it intends to use customer data for future promotions and obtained the express permission of visitors that it can use their names for this purpose. It should also make it possible for visitors to have their names taken off the list on demand at any future date. A further minor point is to ensure that the special offer is legal in all the countries the company does business with, as the law often differs from region to region when it comes to sales promotion and trading offers.

> *MK Music Centre advertises a grand piano for £50 on its Web site. This is a mistake as they normally retail for £5,000. The error only becomes apparent when orders in excess of £1 million are received within a few days.*

The fact that this error occurred on the Web does not change the fact that the retailer is only offering customers the opportunity to buy and is not bound to deliver the goods, even if they have accepted a credit card payment. However, MK Music Centre should route all enquiries by e-mail to its stock control and pricing software so that it does not automatically accept all orders by e-mail unless they have been checked. Auto-confirmation by e-mail is not always a good idea as errors do happen. One way to avoid such problems is to take some time to state clearly the terms and conditions of business, especially the level of liability in cases of error. The program should be written in such a way that the customer has to make a positive 'click' to accept the terms and conditions before an order can be accepted.

The Distance Selling Regulations

The Distance Selling Regulations are designed to implement EC Directive 97/7 on the protection of consumers with regard to distance selling. By implication and in practice this includes e-commerce. The definition of a 'distance sale' is 'any contract... between a supplier and a consumer... which makes exclusive use of one or more means of distant communication up to and including the moment at which the contract is concluded'. A consumer can be a business consumer as well as a private individual. There are some exceptions such as land disposals, vending machines, auctions, financial services or supplying groceries, for example. For most e-business owners though, this means the regulations apply whenever you take orders over the telephone or the Internet. For more details about the Distance Selling Directive, read *Kick-starter.com*, details of which are the back of this book.

Terms and conditions

Most of the provisions can be dealt with in your terms and conditions. At the very minimum you should refer to the following points:

- tell consumers of their right to cancel the order within seven days;
- quote the full price, including delivery and taxes;
- provide comprehensive information about the goods in a durable format;
- the seller must refund any payments received within 30 days if the contract is properly cancelled;
- the seller must deliver the goods within 30 days.

This all sounds eminently sensible and would be best practice anyway if you intend to stay in business for the long term. However, there are some anomalies that have not been addressed by the legislation. If the consumer cancels the contract in accordance with the regulations you are bound by the regulations to refund any monies within the 30 days even though the consumer may not have returned the goods to you. It is not yet clear whether sending an e-mail to a consumer is deemed to be in 'durable format', although in practice this is how most e-businesses are currently complying with this aspect of the law as they are relying on the consumer to print it off as a paper record.

A more worrying aspect of the current wording is the lack of clarity regarding the cooling-off period. In a worst case scenario a consumer could order goods but then cancel the order within seven days. But during that period the goods may have already been dispatched and received by the consumer. It is not clear what the supplier's rights would be concerning the costs of recovery of the goods and the value of the goods themselves which would, by then, have been properly cancelled.

The law on linking

All good Web sites include a number of links to other non-competitive sites to act as a service for visitors. At present no consent is required by law to make such links on your site, although common courtesy might suggest that you should at the very least inform the linked Web site what you have done.

Although the American Bar Association's Commerce in Cyberspace Sub-committee has recently stated that it is not necessary to seek permission before establishing a link, there are a growing number of cases where not all links are welcome or obvious to the site visitor.

The Shetland Times case

The Shetland Times case is one of the few examples where the courts have ruled on an alleged e-commerce issue. The Shetland Times is a local newspaper that also runs an abbreviated version of its editions on its Web site, like many publications. An enterprising Web site owner set up a rival site called The Shetland News and borrowed the story headlines from each edition of The Shetland Times and put them on its own front page. When interested readers clicked on The Shetland News story headlines to find out more information, they were linked straight through to The Shetland Times Web site body copy. This is known as 'framing'. Many readers were unaware that they were then reading a totally different newspaper. It was a clear case of 'passing off' (trying to pass off other people's goods as your own).

The Shetland News defence was that it was acting as a cable programme service because it was a Web site rather than a newspaper. This defence failed due to the specific circumstances of the case. But it is clear that the law is still vague on the status of Web sites when it comes to electronic copyright through links.

The Playboy Enterprises case

In the United States an X-rated Web site, Universal Tel-A-Talk, used the Playboy logo on its homepage to indicate a link to the Playboy site without express permission. Playboy sued successfully on the basis that users were likely to be confused into thinking that Playboy had endorsed or were sponsoring the Universal Tel-A-Talk Web site and by implication its organisation. It also managed to prove that its trademarks would be tarnished by such use.

This was more a case of trade mark infringement than premeditated deception, but any new e-business needs to be aware that using famous brand and logo links as part of your Web site requires careful thought before you go public on a worldwide basis.

Abbey National Bank

But things are not always simple. Abbey National, the UK bank and mortgage provider, recently asked several online introducers to take its details off their Web sites, stating that their sites did not comply with the industry code of practice on giving mortgage advice. The Web site owners in question said that the real reason was that Abbey's products were showing up too low down in their comparative tables. Under new regulations to be implemented by the Financial Services Authority, lenders will be held responsible for the advice of their brokers, so adding a link in this way or even mentioning providers in this way could be subject to dispute within the financial services sector. There is no clear-cut answer at present within the current law.

Deep links: the Ticketmaster case

Ticketmaster operates a Web site that allows customers to purchase tickets for a range of sporting and social events. Another company, Tickets.com, does the same but also offers information on how to buy tickets it does not sell. Visitors to its site are referred by links on the site. They go directly to a 'deep' page of the Ticketmaster Web site, bypassing the homepage and the standard terms and conditions agreement.

Ticketmaster claimed that this was breach of copyright. In other words, Tickets.com was presenting Ticketmaster pages as if they were its own by not routing visitors via the Ticketmaster homepage. Although the judge agreed that no deception was involved because the Ticketmaster logo was clearly visible even through this 'deep' link, the claim for copyright infringement was not dismissed because Tickets.com, allegedly, issued false statements about the availability of tickets from Ticketmaster. More crucially the judge ruled that simply providing a link to the terms and conditions on the homepage did not absolve the duty of the Web site owner to prove agreement to those terms before making contracts with customers.

The message from these cases is that simple links that go directly to other company homepages are in most cases perfectly acceptable. Links that bypass the homepage run the risk of a claim for passing off or copyright infringement and should be avoided. As usual with legal issues, if you are concerned there may be a problem you are probably right, so take some advice before you go too far.

The Data Protection Act 1998

Data protection is as much an issue on the Internet as it is in other channels of distribution. This relatively recent law requires businesses that collect and use personal information from customers to be open about its use and allow those customers access to their information for correction or deletion.

The eight principles of privacy give a good indication of the scope of the legislation that applies to all organisations and businesses, however small:

1. data must be fairly and lawfully processed;
2. it should have limited purposes;

3. information should be relevant but not excessive;
4. it should be accurate;
5. data should not be kept longer than necessary;
6. information should be used in accordance with rights;
7. data should be kept in a secure environment;
8. no data should be sent to a country outside the EU.

One of the main points for e-traders is the specific prohibition of 'spamming' (sending unsolicited commercial messages without the consent of the recipient) to the addresses collected. Normally e-businesses will ask for consent as part of the procedure when taking the first order or enquiry from a new customer or visitor. Unsolicited e-mails can be sent but they must be marked as such so that they can be deleted on receipt. You are also obliged to consult opt-out registers regularly if you do use unsolicited mailings as part of your e-marketing strategy.

You can register online as a 'data user' using www.dpr.gov.uk, where you can find guidance on the principles, how to register, your obligations under the Freedom of Information Act and the register of existing data users or 'data controllers' as they are sometimes known.

Electronic signatures

In July 2000 the then President Clinton signed the Electronic Signatures in Global and National Commerce Act with a swipe card that held his digital signature in a chip. From 1 October 2000 it became legal to use the click of a mouse to make legally binding contracts in the United States. Most of the advanced industrialised nations have followed suit with a rash of new legislation, all with the aim of promoting the growth of e-commerce.

In the UK, trading law has been built upon the principle of the verbal or even the implied contract, so signing documentation has only ever been limited to specific transactions such as house purchase and placing bids. The pressure to create an electronic signature has come largely from the EU, where member states still operate mostly in a business environment where signed contracts for any transaction are the norm rather than the exception.

The Electronic Communications Bill in the UK has given the courts the facility to accept digital signatures as legally binding, and several trials are being conducted within the public sector such as Customs and Excise to see how practical they are for such items as VAT and other business taxes. The Post Office is in the process of handing out free digital signatures to millions of consumers in a bid to increase the security of online transactions. A CD ROM is provided which consumers use to create their own unique set of identifying features that are then encrypted and registered.

It remains to be seen how digital signatures will fit into all the other initiatives currently under way for businesses to be able to verify and authenticate the identity of e-business customers. The plan is that they will soon become as acceptable as a credit card is now for doing business on a remote basis.

Internet misuse by employees

The final area in which legal issues may impact on your new e-business is your staff. Their use or rather their possible misuse of e-mail and the Internet could be a serious issue from a legal point of view. Abuse of the new technology can fall into a number of legal categories:

- time-wasting;
- downloading unsuitable material;
- defamation;
- domain name registrations fraud.

Time-wasting

An Employment Tribunal was asked to judge whether an employee was unfairly dismissed after having searched about 150 sites on her PC during office hours to book a holiday. The employee was found guilty of misconduct and the employer's complaint was upheld. The legal justification was theft of the company's time and misuse of resources.

Downloading unsuitable material

Taking pornographic material from the Web may not in itself be a crime, but sending it to other people may well be. For that reason employers should be aware that they might be vicariously liable for discrimination or an offence under the Obscene Publications Act if one employee sends pornography to another employee.

Merrill Lynch

Merrill Lynch, the investment bank, recently sacked 15 London employees for sending offensive material using the company's e-mail system. A spokesman for the company said that some junior employees were engaged in downloading and then sending racist and pornographic material to other employees, which is strictly prohibited under its guidelines for electronic communications. The downloading was picked up automatically by protection software that detects large quantities of skin tones. There are less sophisticated programs that can screen out certain types of Web site to help employers manage their downloading policy.

Defamation

Employees who send libellous messages to other employees can be prosecuted under the law of defamation. But in some cases the employer could be prosecuted for not taking sufficient care to prevent it happening or ignoring it, thereby harming the reputation of the aggrieved employee.

Both Norwich Union and British Gas have had to pay substantial damages to employees because of defamatory mail received from its own employees. Chevron Oil in the United States had to pay $2.2 million in damages when lawyers found sexist jokes on the internal e-mail system while they were investigating a case of sexual harassment.

Domain name registrations fraud

Less malicious but equally if not more costly could be the case of an employee registering a domain name for your company in his or her own name. If they leave your employment they could take the right to use that domain name with them and so start up as a rival with a valuable trading asset already under their belt. One way to prevent this without going to court is to ensure that all domain names are registered under the company name in the first place.

It has been found that around 60 per cent of Web-linked organisations allow employees access to the Internet but only 20 per cent publish clear guidelines about what is permissible. It helps to avoid confusion if you publish a policy about 'acceptable use' of the Internet by employees, which they should read in the same way that new employees are asked to read the staff handbook in a traditional company.

The new Human Rights Act, which came into force in 2000 in the UK, gives employees the right to keep personal correspondence private if it is received at work. But in the same year the government also issued employers with wide powers to read all employees mail, including e-mail, as part of the Regulation of Investigatory Powers Act, on the basis that it was abuse of the company's assets. This is an ongoing issue which will need to be resolved, but for the moment you could do worse if you are a small business employer than to download the code of practice and draft working agreement model drawn up by the Manufacturing, Science and Finance Union, which aims to present sensible policy guidelines for employers to use in this grey area of legislation (www.msf.itpa.org.uk).

The case law on Internet misuse is still very small and sketchy, but as e-commerce grows it is likely to become more rather than less of an issue, so taking time to draft a workable policy before you start is a sound investment.

Get professional help

Unless there is a specific problem, many small businesses never need to use the legal profession and trade quite happily for many years, relying, perhaps, on their trade association to sort out any points of law that may arise. However, e-business has few precedents that can be relied upon to be able to guess what is legally right. If in doubt, try to remove or avoid the possibility of a problem before you start trading by getting sound advice, particularly if your e-business is your first business. The rules for traditional businesses still apply to e-commerce, even though you may not recognise it in the current case law.

E-business action plan	Useful cyber links
Choose your domain name with care	www.afti.org.uk
Draft your terms and conditions	www.solicitors-online.com
Include Web links with care	www.iab.net
Devise a staff policy on Internet usage	www.do-business.co.uk

7

Marketing your e-business

Let's assume you are happy with your Web site. You have been testing it with a group of friends or colleagues for a few months and it now works properly. You are confident you can deliver your products successfully and collect payment for online orders. You've checked the legal issues. You have your team lined up. You are open for business and all you need now are some customers.

Driving customers to your Web site is a marketing task. You need to draw up a marketing plan to get customers to visit your site: they will not get there by chance. The plan should certainly include collecting buyers' names so that you can get them to return at some future date and buy other related products. It goes almost without saying that you should also include some element of research about what your site visitors think of what you are doing so you can do it better. But unlike traditional businesses your customers only exist as electronic data and may well be globally distributed. That means you have to build strong customer relationships with each customer by remote means. You will need a Customer Relationship Management (CRM) strategy to be at the heart of your marketing effort, if your e-business is going to survive the initial launch period.

The big company marketing approach

A recent survey by the Chartered Institute of Marketing revealed that virtually all businesses that turn over in excess of £50 million have a Web site, but they are mostly used to provide information about products and services. Only 25 per cent have the facility for visitors to buy online. This suggests that they are using the Internet to support their brand or collect customer information rather than to sell goods directly. This is known as 'brochure-ware'.

BrandNet produced the first evaluation of UK brand Web sites in 2000 and listed them according to characteristics such as domain location, navigation, content, brand proposition and effectiveness. The top 10 UK Web sites are shown in Table 7.1.

Table 7.1   Top 10 UK Web sites, Brand 2000

Brand		Product
1.	Famous Grouse	Whisky
2.	Persil	Soap powder
3.	Guinness	Beer
4.	Coca-Cola	Soft drink
5.	Nescafé	Coffee
6.	Tango	Soft drink
7.	Ribena	Soft drink
8.	Andrex	Toilet tissue
9.	Pampers	Nappies
10.	Colgate	Toothpaste

Source: BrandNet

From this list it is clear that larger companies use Web sites to support their consumer products, which are still mainly sold through the retail network. One or two provide incentives such as vouchers to encourage customers to purchase goods perhaps more quickly than they would normally, or to try out new products. Not all by any means, even in this top 10, attempt to collect visitor information or offer links to related sites.

Advertising Web sites through traditional means, such as posters, the press, radio and television has been restricted to a discreet mention somewhere of the World Wide Web address and more explicitly in direct marketing pieces.

Big companies are using their Web sites increasingly for announcing new products or product-related events (42 per cent, 1999; 68 per cent, 2000) but in general the big business model is for the consumer to buy retail in the traditional manner, mainly because transaction values are too low to sell such products direct. Web sites are simply another way to advertise their products. Some commentators think that direct sales from the Internet will only ever reach about 10 per cent of all retail purchases, so large companies cannot abandon their traditional sales routes in the near future, if ever.

Large Internet companies

Internet service providers and global Web-based businesses have become almost a byword for overt marketing expenditure, which leads the budding e-preneur to wonder whether to be a success in e-business you have to spend a lot of money on advertising. 'Cash-burning' seems to be endemic amongst the bigger Web sites, with the hope that once the name is established and visitors have been attracted to the site, revenues will start to flow. But as one spectacular failure follows another it is clear that not all Web sites are the same in funding and marketing terms. Each company has its own unique set of circumstances that require the Web site owners to think through exactly what marketing would be appropriate for them.

Advertising is not the only answer

To a non-specialist trying to get a foothold in the Internet users market, mass advertising would appear to be the answer to driving consumers to your new site. But recent research by WebProbe, a media research company, discovered that less than 1 per cent of TV viewers visited Web sites as a result of seeing them advertised on television. This compared with 13 per cent for newspaper advertisements and 15 per cent for word of mouth. This finding is also supported by the fall in revenues recorded by the top 24 UK dot.coms, from £111 million to around £80 million (1999/2000). The moral seems to be that if you have deep pockets and have a lot of funding or an established national or international brand, television advertising is the quickest way to get market share of consumer awareness of your Web site. But it does not necessarily lead to enough Internet sales to justify the cost and is probably not right for small businesses.

The small-company marketing approach

The marketing needs of smaller companies are much more practical as they rarely have a well-known consumer brand to protect or a large distribution network to sell through. For an e-business owner the key issue is finding customers to sell products to and getting paid. This involves at the very least letting potential customers know you exist.

Traditionally a small business uses catalogue mailings, leaflet door drops, local advertising, trade advertising, specialist magazines, telesales and the occasional exhibition to create a presence. If you are a franchisee you may benefit from regional or national advertising. There is no reason why any if not all of these marketing avenues cannot be exploited to get your Web site known. Even an advertisement in *Yellow Pages* or a local businesses directory could carry your Web site address. But the number of visitors to your site through these channels is likely to be tiny compared to the numbers you will need to make your e-business viable on an ongoing basis.

The key issue for Web site-only companies is how to shepherd online users to your site using the existing marketing channel you both share – the Internet. For small companies the marketing challenge revolves around search engines and how to get the best out of them by embedding keywords in your site text that major search engines will look for and by keeping a careful eye on your rank position in each one. All the other marketing media, both Web-based and the more traditional media that you can employ to spread the word, are clearly useful and supportive, but if you neglect search engines you will never get your e-business off the ground.

Search engines

When people go online they have a choice of around 800 million pages to look at. Unless you have spent several years and lots of money creating a demand for your Web site, like Amazon.com for example, potential visitors are unlikely to think of you by chance or even remember your Web address correctly, if they are looking just for your site. To help users find what they are looking for on the Web, there are specialist indexing companies called 'search engines'. The most widely known include Yahoo!, Ask Jeeves (see Figure 7.1), Excite, Lycos, Google and AltaVista. Most of them have global reach but there are increasing numbers of search engines that are country-specific, which helps because they tend to direct you to more local sources of information.

Search engines are software programs that scour the pages of the Web to catalogue and index any new pages and all the existing ones. When you type in a keyword or phrase they will find all the Web sites that contain those keywords in their text. The customer simply clicks through to your site on a link. However, the marketing problem becomes evident when you discover that the search engine has found 3,000 sites that mention the customer's keyword. If you

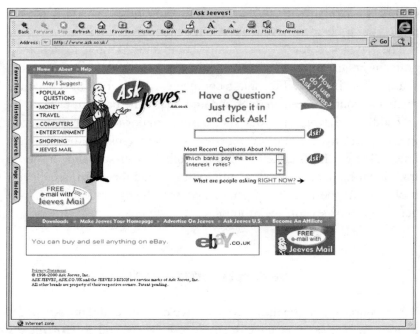

Figure 7.1 Search engine example: Ask Jeeves

are number 2,999 on the list of useful Web sites you may as well be invisible.

The customer's viewpoint

As many as 80 per cent of all searches on the Internet begin using search engines, so as a means of getting noticed by new customers they cannot be ignored.

From a marketing perspective you need to think what your potential customers are likely to look for and how they will conduct their search. If they know your Web site name they will probably just type that in, but if it is an unremarkable name that could be spelt wrongly (like ABC/A.B.C./AB&C services) they may be sent hundreds of references and may never find your specific site. If they do not know your name but are looking for companies that provide what you provide, such as sausages for example, you could also find yourself amongst hundreds of entries including sausage machine manufacturers.

The trick is to think pedantically and try to enter your Web site address with specific keywords that can lead customers to you and perhaps only half a dozen others with similar businesses. In general the fewer keywords there are the wider the search, so it is always better to define what you do very accurately in, say, three or four keywords. That way your main target audience will find you much more easily. For example, if you sell handmade chairs you need to register your keywords with the search engines as 'antique, reproduction wooden chairs' rather than just 'furniture'. One tip is to group words together between quotation marks as a total phrase, if you know it is a phrase that customers would use, as this will narrow the search dramatically.

Another characteristic to bear in mind is that most search engines are US in origin, which is fine if you want customers from the United States. But to help UK customers you may want to register as a UK site in the search engine's UK section or better still register with a UK search engine, such as UK Plus. You should also bear in mind that no single search engine covers the entire Web. Even the biggest, FAST (www.alltheweb.com) only scans 300 million pages. Customers may use three or four different search engines on a regular basis to find sites, so you need to be registered with several simply to cover the ground.

In terms of marketing planning you need to bear in mind that getting your site to appear on a search engine could take as long as eight weeks from submission, so do not plan your launch timetable until you are sure you have been listed.

For more details about how search engines work and what you need to do to make them a more effective marketing tool, visit www.search enginewatch.com.

How to get registered

Registering your Web site with relevant search engines can be done online for a small fee or even for free through Internet marketing sites like Exploit or Submit. They will ask you to send a short (10 or 20 words) and a long description of your site; remember to write in three or four key words that the search software can look for. Try and include one or more of them in your title. The details are then passed on to a dozen or so of the leading search engine sites. You can pay a little more to have them sent to all the search engines on the Web. In marketing terms the extra cost is well worth it, so do not stint in getting your name out into the marketplace. You can also do this piecemeal directly with each of the major search engines, which would give you the opportunity to tailor your entry to each search engine, but it does take a long time.

You should test the major search engines on a regular basis to see how high you are ranked using your keywords. A service called Position Agent can check where you are and, depending on your position, you may then decide to change your keywords to get a higher listing.

A recent innovation has been the appearance of sites that can help you improve your position in the rankings on a regular basis. Site owners say that you need to be in the top 20 of any list for new customers to find you. WebPosition Gold, created by FirstPlace Software, offers to push you up the rankings of search engines through clever algorithms, watching the changes in the rank order of competitive sites on a regular basis and careful analysis of your keywords. They claim to be able to save Web site owners over 30 hours a week of checking, through a one-off charge for their software of around £100. If it actually drives visitors to your site the cost is insignificant in the long run.

One good thing about search engines and the Internet in general, unlike traditional advertising, is that you can count up each week how many visitors came to your site and how they got there. Such data is very valuable in helping you decide which search engines to concentrate on when it comes to improving your presence or investing in some additional paid-for advertising.

Online advertising

If you have mentioned your new Web site on all your literature and stationery and managed to get relatively high rankings on your targeted search engines, you may well consider online advertising as another way to increase potential visitors to your site. An example is shown in Figure 7.2.

Figure 7.2 Online advertising

Banner ads

Banner ads are the most popular form of online advertising and typically take the shape of a horizontal graphical bar showing a logo or the name of the company doing the advertising. Sometimes they are animated. Normally banner ads provide a link to the sponsor's Web site by the visitor clicking on the banner ad.

Text ads

Text ads do a similar job but tend to consist of copy or text if the proposition is too complex for a banner ad. It often carries an e-mail link.

Interstitials

These are advertisements that appear between Web pages when you are browsing a site. They need to be well designed and appropriate as slow download times can be irritating for visitors who will be engaged looking for something else when the interstitial appears.

Pop-ups

As you might expect, pop-ups pop-up in small windows during a browser session, ideally with something relevant to say to the browsing visitor.

HTML and rich media ads

Usually full page, this type of ad uses text, graphics and other HTML features to provide a complete sponsor's message as part of someone else's Web site. Rich media ads often include snippets of video to support any online message, or interactive competitions to encourage visitors to stay on the site a little longer than they normally would.

Sponsorship

Less intrusive is the sponsorship of sites, where an inactive branding device lets visitors know that the site has the support of a non-competitive party.

Should you advertise?

Online advertising is in its infancy as a medium to influence purchasers. The costs can look relatively low. A banner ad could be as little as £20 per thousand impressions. But the key issue is effectiveness, as it is with all your marketing spend. The 'click-through' rate for most banner ads from UK visitors is only about half of 1 per cent. By clicking-through, visitors are expressing an interest but they are not necessarily going to buy from you or look at your site in any detail. That said, Internet advertising is set to grow rapidly in the next five years, as you can see from Table 7.2.

Table 7.2 Global online advertising predictions (US $, billions)

	1999	2000	2001	2002	2003
United States	3.5	5.4	7.4	9.8	12.2
Europe	0.43	0.91	1.5	2.3	3.1
Asia	0.23	0.50	0.88	1.4	1.9
Latin America	0.05	0.13	0.24	0.40	0.63
Aus/NZ	0.02	0.07	0.14	0.21	0.29
Other	0.01	0.28	0.61	0.12	0.21
Total	4.24	7.29	10.77	14.23	18.33

Source: Jupiter Media Matrix, 2000

From this table it is clear that Internet advertising is set to quadruple at the very least, but most of the spend will be in the United States, with Europe a long way behind. When you consider the market share of

Internet advertising compared with traditional advertising, the proportion will only be around 6 per cent. It suggests that Web-based advertising may not be enough to get the required numbers to your site, so you need to think of even more ways to get attention.

Banner ads analysis

A German Internet company recently analysed the business impact of Internet banner advertising, looking at the behaviour of 500 Internet users in the UK, Germany, France, Sweden and Spain. In most cases banner advertising was perceived to have good informational value and to be an easy way to get access to the advertiser's Web site. Up to 48 per cent of the sample described banner advertising as the 'advertising medium of the future'. So, if you do any advertising on the Internet at all it would seem to make sense to start with banners.

Many ISPs offer Web site visitor analysis as part of their hosting package. There are a number of tools that can be downloaded, depending on what you want to know. Netlink provides raw Unix data that are easy to read and analyse. Direct Connection allows you to see your data as text or graphics. BT Internet tells you how to get hold of free analysis tools like Webtrends to help you monitor your online marketing. It can tell you how many 'hits' you received over any period, although this should only be seen as a general measure of your marketing effectiveness. More important for your marketing planning is how your visitors actually move around your Web site and what they look at and, of course, how many buy anything. Ten thousand hits a week is of no use whatsoever if they all leave your site on a reciprocal link after 20 seconds and never get to your order form page. In October 2000 the food site, foodoo.com, which was backed by a number of famous TV chefs, was recording 11,500 hits a week on its site. By November it had run out of revenue and went into receivership.

Comparing the costs

Whenever you consider paid-for advertising you need to know the comparative costs of different types of other advertisements. Your overall plan may be to become a household name through your new e-business, but buying the exposure that will drive visitors to your Web site can be expensive. Consider the comparative costs of using traditional media and a simple homepage banner ad on a major portal to run for three or four weeks:

Homepage banner ad, major portal	£40,000
Black-and-white, full-page national press ad	£90,000
30-second radio ad	£380,000
30-second cinema ad	£870,000
National poster campaign	£910,000
Bus-stop poster campaign	£1,300,000
30-second national TV ad	£4,400,000

From this it is clear that paying for a banner ad on a major portal is relatively inexpensive compared with a national television commercial, although £40,000 is still a large amount of investment for a small business. Depending on your type of business you may want to launch your site with such a banner ad and perhaps the purchase of relevant keywords on one or two search engines for a short time to get exposure during the early stages of your campaign.

There may come a time when paid-for, traditional advertising makes good commercial sense. Local radio, for example, could be a cost-effective way to reach your particular market if what you sell online has a local dimension. But it is more likely that you will have to make use of all the complementary and low-cost deals the Internet has to offer before you go spending tens of thousands to get national awareness for your site.

Free online marketing

If banner advertising is the most effective type of advertising, why not consider reciprocal links where you approach another site owner and swap banner ads with a linking capability? You could share any revenue generated from either site so that the arrangement is not one-sided. The tools mentioned above should help you determine how many visitors clicked through on each site in any given period.

You might approach another site owner with a co-branding idea of complementary services, such as a shoes supplier and a socks supplier. The site could be designed in such a way that the offer appears to be equally balanced, featuring both parties to the same degree. Revenues could either be shared or you take your shoes revenue and your partner takes their socks revenue.

You could take an active part in 'newsgroups'. These are online discussion groups of which there are tens of thousands on the Internet, with new ones springing up every day. Word of mouth is a powerful marketing tool, especially if you have a niche product. Hobby sites use newsgroups to great effect because enthusiasts will recommend a good product in the context of an open discussion, which is much more effective an endorsement than a paid-for commercial. Anyone can post a message to the newsgroup. Often the best way to get started is to suggest your product as an answer or part answer to someone else's problem. But do not be too pushy. The value of newsgroups is to let the visitors do the selling for you. To see if there is a newsgroup relevant to what you do, visit www.dejanews.com or ask your ISP.

Web rings are loose alliances between Web sites that link complementary services with each other in a ring of five or six sites. They could be customers with mutual interests, suppliers with complementary products or specialised directories. Each Web site carries a link to the others at no charge to any party. Contact www.webring.com to see how you can form your own Web ring group to raise your profile.

Providing an e-mail facility for visitors as part of your Web site is another way to market your services and keep the marketing effort going. Subject to their consent, you can use those addresses later on to send them details of other products or run interactive competitions or prize draws on a regular basis. Or you could create your own newsgroup if your product lends itself to a type of 'online club' and get visitors to recruit other members to swell its ranks. Again, your ISP may be able to help you organise it at no charge.

Ministry of Sound/Funplanet case history

Ministry of Sound cooperated with Funplanet, a Swedish games Web site, to offer online games and activities for visitors such as music trivia quizzes, which encourage stays on average of up to 10 minutes at a time. Funplanet wanted to get more exposure to a specific group of potential customers and paid Ministry of Sound around £35,000 in return for guaranteed traffic through the Ministry of Sound Web site links. The Funplanet site sold advertising on its site and some of that revenue also went back to the Ministry of Sound. In its first three months of operation, the Ministry of Sound site delivered over 1,200 visitors to the Funplanet site and collected over 400 registrations which were then used later on by both parties for direct marketing of their own non-competing products.

Although in the Funplanet case substantial costs were involved, the elements of mutual benefit from marketing cooperation and creativity are evident. You could take the principles of this cooperation and approach another site owner and see if it might work without any revenue changing hands at all. The only restrictions are what each side finds commercially acceptable.

Online games

One of the more common marketing buzz words when it comes to Web site development is creating a 'sticky' site. In essence this means providing reasons for visitors to stay on the site and provide you with more details about their buying habits, which you can use later on for marketing purposes. One of the more common ways to get visitors to stay online is to create a game. Clearly it needs to be relevant to the profile of your visitors, but just because you may sell business to business does not mean that using games is out of the question.

Clients of The Games Kitchen (www.gameskitchen.com) which provides games for corporate Web sites, include a recruitment company and a law firm. *The Times* has an online Times Crossword with substantial cash prizes, but in essence it is a game. The dos and don'ts include not making it too complex, making it easy to download and having a plan to promote it on other parts of your site. Online games can be leased for short periods from game development specialists, but even outright purchase can be as little as £1,000.

E-mail marketing

Marketing by sending e-mail messages is the fastest-growing Internet marketing activity and certainly one of the most efficient. Current average click-through rates in the United States are about 12 per cent, with sales in some sectors running at 2.5 per cent, which is certainly higher than traditional direct marketing. The incidence of sending inappropriate e-mail messages has been low. Some say the average online user receives less than one per week, which means for the time being there is a distinct novelty value in being approached 'cold' via e-mail. Many communications can be automatically triggered by the users' behaviour and so it requires relatively little intervention once the system has been set up. But just as with direct mail, consumer groups are already actively lobbying for tighter controls over e-mail marketing, so registering with the appropriate industry body and abiding by its principles could be a smart move, if only to understand the privacy issues involved.

All these types of activity can be quite time-consuming when done properly. You may find it worthwhile to assign one of your junior technical people, if you have any, to take responsibility for it, as well as keeping the Web site up-to-date and answering e-mails. Prompt replies and well-run cooperative deals help to build confidence in your site and a good site will get talked about. Being a Webmaster, as they are known, is fast becoming a recognised career path for software programmers, so finding such people is no longer as difficult as it used to be. Most recruitment agencies will have 'Webmasters' on their database of job hunters.

Free offline marketing

Just because you are setting up an online business you should not neglect other more established marketing tools. As well as branding all your marketing materials with your new e-business references, you should consider more traditional PR techniques to get your Web site noticed.

For a small business that does not have the luxury of a specific PR budget, there is a lot you can do yourself to spread the word about your e-business. Trade and hobby magazines are often 'copy light' if they produce regular issues, so they are almost certain to print details of your new e-business provided it can be presented as relevant to the readership. You might even suggest a short article on the main issues you faced in setting up your e-business and an update on how things are going now.

There is a growing number of computer and e-business magazines that are widely read by just the type of site visitor you are hoping to attract. You could do worse than submit your site to them for a Web site review, but do ensure it works properly before you take the plunge.

Local newspapers are often keen to print details of local businesses doing something different, particularly in weekly business supplements or special reports. Case histories always go down well, but remember to feature the name of your Web site several times and ask to check that they have got it right before they go to press. Good coverage with the wrong Web address is not much use to you from a marketing perspective.

The integrated approach

No single marketing technique will deliver thousands of visitors to your site on a consistently regular basis. If there was a sure-fire way to do that it would probably be a money-spinning Web site in its own right.

The experience of successful new e-businesses has been that the most effective plans involve using all of the free services, with a judicious spend on more traditional techniques and banner advertising, if you have any promotional budget left. Direct mail has a specific role to play as your potential visitors may be clearly defined in a niche market and their names and addresses probably already exist on a commercial list. One example is British Airways, which combined traditional direct mail to the 1 million members of its frequent flyer club with follow-up reminders by e-mail. Twenty per cent of the recipients subsequently logged on to the Web site to check out the deals being offered, in a direct mail market where a 2 or 3 per cent response rate is the norm.

The large ISPs have tended to use brand advertising on television to get awareness, then followed it up with giveaway CD ROMs in local newspapers or national magazines, depending on their target market. So it is worth considering a two-stage approach to gathering new names, starting with more traditional marketing activities to get broad awareness, followed up by targeted, direct action.

Turning visitors into a database

The final word on marketing techniques must be about the whole question of why you are trying to drive all those visitors to your site in the first place. This is not simply to get sales. The overriding objective of an e-business is to build a database of visitors and customers to whom you can sell and sell again for many years to come. Large companies call this process Customer Relationship Management or CRM. More details of how you might create a strategy for your e-business based on CRM principles are given in Chapter 10.

Realising that all your marketing should be driven by the need to create a long-term relationship with your customers allows you to make the right decisions on expenditure in the early days and the level of investment you will need as the years go by. The likelihood is that you will get many more 'hits' than you originally expected but many fewer sales. But your online customers will be intensely loyal if you treat them well and will produce much higher profits than an average customer buying from you in the traditional, non-e way.

E-business action plan	Useful cyber links
Decide whether you should brand or sell	www.advalue.co.uk
Plan your search engine strategy	www.searchenginewatch.com
Is online advertising feasible?	www.valueclick.com
Take advantage of free advertising	www.webring.com

8

E-business and your back-office

Nearly 95 per cent of all goods and services purchased by corporations are purchased with paper-based processes.

Walid Mougayer, Opening Digital Markets, 1998

By now you will be fully aware of all the front-end things you need to do to get a credible e-business off the ground. But if it cannot deliver the goods because the back-up administration is poor, then you have no e-business at all. It may be that you should not take the risk of upsetting those early customers by automating your entire business process and making mistakes. Not everyone does try to automate everything from the beginning. In fact the majority of e-businesses only use part of the new technology in the initial stages, opting to add electronic back-office automation such as procurement at a later stage when they are confident it will work well.

A recent survey of AIM listed companies by accountants Pannell Kerr Foster showed that although 90 per cent of companies surveyed used their Web site to improve their public profile, only 20 per cent were actively engaged in using the site to procure supplies. Most businesses with a Web site are therefore not using its full potential and are taking the gradual approach.

Examples of the gradual approach

Homepro... providing a point of contact

Homepro.com is a Web site for anyone looking for a plumber, a painter or a fence-builder to come and do some work on their home. Homepro checks and screens 5,000 trades people and matches its list against your requirements. It shortlists the best qualified specialists in the customer's area and they are given the customer's name, telephone number and address. Through the site contact is made and arrangements about when to call are usually made over the 'phone. The Internet advantage is the ability to find quickly reputable trades people who live in the customer's area. In this case the Web site is being used like a directory. The actual trading is done in the usual way.

Top Jobs... matching job-seekers to vacancies

Top Jobs runs a Web site that receives over 200,000 'hits' a month from job-seekers. Clients are asked to give brief details of the kind of vacancy they are looking for over the Internet. The Top Jobs software matches their position to the database and automatically sends them an e-mail with the relevant vacancies listed. Job-seekers can then e-mail Top Jobs or ring up to make an appointment. The service is much cheaper for recruiters than using press advertisements, and once the search element is over Top Jobs does its normal recruiting job in the traditional way.

The Provender delicatessen... partially interactive, national site

The Wessex Provender is a retail Web site that began life in response to a failed direct marketing exercise. Delicatessen owner Roger Biddle was convinced he could get more customers by doing a local direct marketing campaign. As it turned out his mailing to 500 people within a five mile radius of the shop only pulled in five orders and was very expensive. With the help of a program called Shop@ssistant devised by The Floyd Consultancy, he put all his products online. But due to the expense he did not set up any secure systems to take cash and simply asked customers to ring or fax their credit card number or send a cheque. After a year he now takes about one confirmed order a week, but online orderers tend to spend three times as much as retail customers. On average there are about 60 visitors a week to the site.

The wedding company... fully interactive, global site

Wedding List Services employed 15 people and turned over around £1 million in wedding gifts from people visiting its premises or using mail order in 1999. However, there were a significant number of potential purchasers who could not visit the shop and many lived abroad. The company decided to invest in a fully interactive Web site (www.wedding.co.uk) that could offer a much wider range of gifts than, say, the local department store or even Harrods, and undertake the transactions even if the customer and the guests to the wedding lived overseas. The site cost £14,000 to set up. Customers and present-givers get access the site by a password and choose from over 40,000 gifts, with the money being taken by credit card on a secure system. The site owner admits it will never replace the core business but reckons within five years it could account for about half of the company's entire revenue.

The point of these simple examples is to show that not everyone needs to go down the entire route of e-business in one sudden leap. Many retailers do not have the cash to invest in expensive, do-everything sites from the beginning and in many cases this is very shrewd as the take-up can be quite low in terms of numbers. But others have discovered that they have a truly global market and unless they offer the entire e-business package they risk not taking full advantage of their original idea.

However, once they get beyond a certain size and are perhaps more comfortable with what the Internet can offer, many small businesses realise that the true value of going online is that they can now trade electronically with their suppliers by linking directly with their systems. This is known as e-procurement and is set to become by far the most significant change in the way business is done since the Industrial Revolution.

Procurement: a short history

Other than pure consultancies, most businesses make their profits from buying in raw materials, adding value through the production process and selling on those enhanced materials to the waiting market.

From EDI to today

Electronic Data Interchange or EDI has been around for some 20 years or more, particularly within the engineering, retail and financial markets. But most large companies remember the days when couriers would be sending large boxes of magnetic tape up and down the country on motorbikes so that vital files could be viewed by other parts of the business or by suppliers. But as soon as two computers were linked up for commercial gain the possibility of data exchange without the need for 'human' intervention became apparent. In the early days only text could be exchanged, but with the advent of the World Wide Web HTML language and Mosaic in the early 1990s, both text and graphics could be sent to remote locations. General Electric was an early pioneer with its Trading Post electronic procurement application.

By 1995 the Common Gateway Interface (CGI) had been developed, which allowed static data to become interactive through dynamic client/server applications. For the first time remote businesses could query files, change specifications, send attached e-mails and use other software to manipulate other people's data files. In short, CGI allowed virtually all businesses connected to the World Wide Web to be able to check stock levels, order goods, check the identity of the other business and receive payments on an electronic basis at great speed.

The third phase was the emergence of XML – eXtensible Markup Language. XML is a standard, generalised language for the structured storage and transfer of information on the Internet. The big advantage of using XML as a programming language is the ability to translate virtually any file in whatever format to any other format. The significance for e-commerce is that there is now a simpler way for businesses to exchange both text and graphical information, which should enable even small businesses to compete in the wider world of the Internet.

Large buyers are now using the new technology to create their own private intranet exchanges to manage their buying processes. Tesco supermarket has developed its own EDI system into which 1,300 suppliers have been enrolled. The system now accounts for 96 per cent of all Tesco's purchases. Considerable pressure was put on suppliers to have the necessary interface to be able to supply goods online rather than through a paper-based system. Commerce One pioneered the idea of offering B2B buyers a user-friendly marketplace with its BuySite application. The idea was for large businesses not to build up their own procurement software at all but for specific industries to support a single buying system that everyone could use. The more companies using the system the lower the prices, in theory.

Procurement for small businesses

The next step was to make business exchange software available to everyone, not only the large companies. Just a few years ago small traders were excluded from any kind of commercially viable data interchange because the software development costs were so great. ASPs (Application Service Providers) have changed all that. ASPs provide data manipulation software online. That means you use it when you need to and have no maintenance or ongoing costs. One of the most prominent ASPs on the market is my mysap.com. The application takes the existing SAP enterprise resource planning software and converts it into a Web format. Users can buy and sell goods, form partnerships and participate in those important newsgroups within their own vertical market.

AOL, the well-known ISP, has teamed up with Purchasepro.com to provide small businesses with all the software they need to conduct efficient data exchange without the high costs of developing their own software. The Purchasepro software allows business users to make bids for contracts online and negotiate terms. A key feature of the package is the use of AOL Instant Messenger technology, which creates two-way communication between participants to enable deals to be achieved more efficiently.

E-bay, the auction site, has also entered the small business market with a business exchange system aimed at servicing organisations with less than 100 employees. The current application allows small businesses to buy and sell products online in 34 separate business categories.

ASPs provide packaged software applications, professional services, computing hardware and network connections, all for a monthly fee. They differ from ISPs in that they provide virtually all of your e-commerce development, but you may need to be prepared to sign a longer-term contract than you would with an ISP.

One of the key issues for a small business is whether you actually need all the services the ASP can supply. If you need an online retail facility you need to look at several alternatives and check that you really will use all the features they offer. You may need to have a few meetings with the service provider to check over terms and conditions and get some reassurance that they can really deliver what they say they can. In particular you should ask them about any service agreement details as you will need them to be on call if things go wrong or to remedy any problems if there is any downtime. At the moment there is a lot of choice, but it is likely that the market will consolidate and some ASPs will not be able to maintain the levels of service currently being offered. Tying yourself up with an ASP that eventually goes under could be disastrous for your e-business, as all you have is data. If your data disappears with the ASP you will have no e-business to speak of.

Another aspect that will help a small business decide to go down the ASP route is the need to trade securely. Setting up secure payment systems and the necessary 'firewalls' to protect your own system from unwanted intrusion or malicious hackers from the Internet is expensive to do by yourself. Even your most hopeful business plan is unlikely to be able to absorb this development cost out of first or second year sales.

Bringing EDI right up to date, it is fair to say that the arrival of ASPs has made it possible for the first time for small enterprises to get large company deals with suppliers by joining in with other small businesses through one of the many business exchange sites. Even if your Web site does not initially generate vast numbers of customer orders, by being linked to the Internet for procurement you could save considerable sums of money by buying direct. It may even result in having less overhead tied up in dealing with suppliers, which will enable you to concentrate even more on marketing your site to the waiting world.

E-business action plan	Useful cyber links
Consider my back-office routines	www.wilsonweb.com
Is the gradual approach right for me?	www.bizmove.com
Learn about the technology of procurement	www.mysap.com
Could I join a suppliers group?	www.usecolor.com

9 *B2B – creating new marketplaces*

Procuring your own supplies is only one part of the story. The whole concept of B2B (business to business) procurement is undergoing a radical shakeout. Perhaps there is a new business idea in it for you within your own industry niche?

It is a well-known fact that B2B use of the Internet will far outstrip the B2C (business to consumer) market over the next five years. Despite the hype in the consumer sector, the real money will be made by business to business companies that find a niche supplying goods and services to other businesses. But it is not just a question of putting your catalogue online and waiting for the orders to roll in. You need to provide an exchange of data so that trade can be done round the clock and instantaneously.

Such Web sites are the newest phase of the Internet, but unlike their consumer counterparts, they can be instantly profitable if they are set up correctly. This chapter deals with the enormous potential of the B2B market, which even small players can enter and be successful at because size is of relatively little importance when you trade on the World Wide Web. The converse is also true. It may not be too many years before big customers will insist on all suppliers having the facility to supply online; they will not place the business without it. That may not matter if you intend to stay small, but few businesses plan strategically not to grow and growth usually comes from finding a few large businesses to sell into.

What is a B2B marketplace?

When commercial buyers and sellers come together to trade products or services, they are usually in physical contact by letter, telephone or in person. With the advent of the new technology, the Internet provides the necessary forum for contact and the exchange of data and prices, so the market becomes virtual. It only exists electronically as messages on a screen. This is what is known as a B2B marketplace. Deloitte Research reckons there are more than 1,400 of them, with about 85 per cent originating in the United States. Analysts also claim that when run efficiently B2B marketplaces can remove around 90 per cent of the administration costs of procurement, so in theory it is a win–win situation for both buyers and suppliers.

Chematch is an example of a vertical B2B marketplace site. It provides an exchange for commodity chemicals where members bid for specific consignments and negotiate online to get the best deal. It has over 500 corporate members but it still needs to employ 80 people in its salesforce to create the leverage for better buying power and to sign up new members.

B2B marketplaces can be horizontal, servicing several markets with a similar product such as spare parts, raw materials or services. Ariba Network, Purchasingcenter and Bizbuyer may be familiar to you if you are an SME.

Others have been set up by a particular industry sector itself to service the needs of all its members. Covisint was formed in February 2000 by cooperation between General Motors, DaimlerChrysler and Ford. Nissan and Renault joined soon after. Covisint acts as a central marketplace for components, supplies and specific industry information and expects to facilitate the sale of items worth over $240 billion a year from thousands of suppliers. The purpose is to take cost out of the supply chain and be able to offer cheaper products to the whole industry. The side benefit is a more efficient industry and a more level playing field for suppliers to compete in, as well as less expensive products for consumers.

Sometimes companies are so big and purchase so many supplies on a regular basis that inventing their own e-procurement business is the only sensible way forward. Just like the Tesco example mentioned in the previous chapter, British Telecom put together its own procurement Web site for its staff to use. Employees can find out which suppliers have items in stock, order the goods, track progress through the buying system and negotiate for the best delivery terms. The average cost of placing a purchase order will be cut from £70 to around £5 once the system is fully operational. One of the main benefits has been to streamline the policy for purchasing, which avoids the possibility of favouritism and in some cases simply unprofessional buying practices.

The small business opportunity

Of more interest to e-business entrepreneurs is setting up your own independent marketplace either as an existing manufacturer or a stand-alone enterprise. General Electric, mentioned in the previous chapter, was one of the first global companies to insist that all its suppliers sell to it online, thereby reducing its inventory and keeping prices competitive. In time such industry or manufacturer inspired companies may be floated off as separate companies to realise their investment value.

However, the majority of B2B marketplaces are a combination of market knowledge and software expertise, which when combined offer an unrivalled expertise of procurement and IT know-how. Automated transactions and the merging of databases of products provide customers with an expanded choice and lower procurement costs. It is reckoned that ordering office stationery, for example, can cost between £100 and £150 if you factor in the traditional administration. By doing it online the cost can be reduced to around £10 per order.

A further sophistication of a B2B marketplace is to auction goods to the highest bidder electronically rather than stick to the catalogue price. The price could, of course, be higher or lower than you were expecting to pay. But it allows suppliers with excess stock to offload it and receive some cash rather than have it tied up in inventory. A variation is the reverse auction in which many suppliers vie to supply a single buyer with goods, which aims to drive prices down and promote competition.

How does anyone in B2B make money if all it does is drive prices down? Some marketplaces charge a subscription fee, which gives 'members' access to the site by means of a password. Others charge a commission or deal fee or take a percentage of the items sold, like an auction house would. Other services are also sold to members such as market reviews, news or other items of information that can be downloaded from the site on a 24/7 (24 hours, seven days a week) basis. Advertising from suppliers is also taken to provide another stream of revenue.

B2B case history – sparesFinder.com

David Stroud is the Operations Director of a B2B marketplace called sparesFinder.com. In 1998 he began to put together the building blocks of a B2B idea that is a classic in every sense. With considerable experience in the City as an analyst, he was aware that there was a global market for engineering spares of around £500 billion. What is more, most companies were prepared to pay over the odds for specific parts if not having them meant getting behind schedule on an important project.

He was also aware that the traditional methods of procurement were costly and inefficient. Most buyers would contact agents or intermediaries through directories or under contracts, who would then use their own contacts in a vertical search system. He was convinced that by applying the right software together with the benefits of connectivity that the Internet brings he could reduce procurement costs for spares by between 10 and 50 per cent. This would leave him with more than enough profit to grow the business further.

The proposition was simple. He would set up sparesFinder.com as an ASP (Application Service Provider) which would link all the disparate systems of buyers and sellers together. Buyers would be able to search the system at any time of the day or night through their own internal intranets or via the Web itself and place orders direct. Revenue would come to sparesFinder by charging an annual subscription fee and through one-off consultancies or market reports. In this way sparesFinder put big buyers in direct contact with the smallest suppliers and vice versa through the Internet. By linking all the possible suppliers together, sparesFinder is able to provide a virtually perfect search facility and arrange for dispatch as efficiently as possible.

The next stage was for competing companies to realise that they could all benefit from an open market for goods, in other words more visibility of both suppliers and purchasers. The ever-widening circles in Figure 9.1 (see page 126) indicate the ever-widening visibility in the marketplace, which in turn leads to lower prices and better value for buyers. Now every buyer and every supplier was known, which created more open competition for goods and services.

By 2000 sparesFinder had over 75 subscribing companies in the areas of oil and gas, power, chemicals, pulp and paper, mining, tobacco and food processing. It has suppliers in over 150 locations drawn from 25 countries. The ongoing task continues to be the recruitment of new suppliers and the search for buyers who will pay the subscription to be connected. As in most e-businesses, the quest for economies of scale is no different to those in a traditional business.

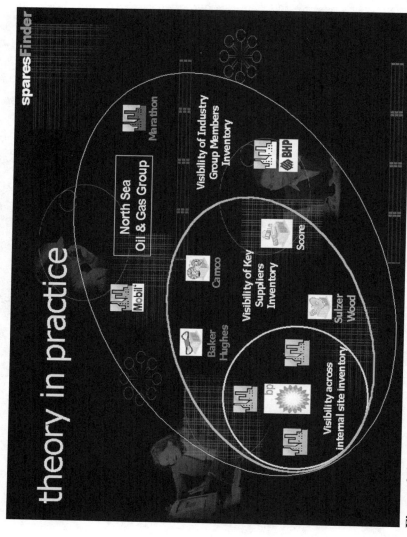

Figure 9.1 Competitors can share the cost benefits of online procurement

Some marketing tips

In a presentation held at Microsoft's UK headquarters, David Stroud offered the following advice to those hoping to start an e-business:

- Find an idea that is different or one that exists but is not done very well.
- Make sure it uses the uniqueness of the Web in some new way.
- Provide what customers want rather than what analysts and consultants advise.
- Focus on the unique offer; don't get sidetracked.
- Is the idea scalable (can it grow bigger)?
- How strongly can you sell the buyers' club idea?
- Don't undersell your service.

From the above description, sparesFinder follows the rules for a successful e-business in that it has found a service gap that could be better filled by using Web technology and it has global applications. In other words it has plenty of room to grow. The application software is not particularly complicated but the idea to apply it to the industrial spares market is all about inspiration and entrepreneurship rather than textbook models.

Implications for the future

The B2B marketplace concept could have a dramatic impact on businesses both large and small over the next five years. There could be a number of ways the lives of smaller businesses could be affected.

Legal issues

It has been and could be argued again that 'buyers clubs' are nothing more than a good old-fashioned cartel. The difference between collaboration and collusion is not great. At the moment both the EC and the US regulatory bodies are taking a benign line in the rush to get businesses online with the minimum of regulatory control. But several B2B deals involving the pooling of an entire industry's purchasing have been examined in some detail. The EC recently ruled in favour of myaircraft.com after some claims that its dominant position in the market was tantamount to full control and restrictive trade.

The two issues a new B2B marketplace may need to consider are whether the sharing of information by competitors could lead to price-fixing or other anti-competitive behaviour within certain industries, and whether there are any restrictions on who can subscribe. Marketplaces need to be open to all potential subscribers if they are to comply with existing anti-trust laws. If anything, the current relaxed mood will strengthen the opportunity for small businesses to be invited to pitch for large contracts where before it would have been virtually unheard of.

Retail suppliers

New B2B marketplaces in retail are springing up all the time. GlobalNetXchange is a joint venture between Sears Roebuck, Carrefour, Sainsbury's, Metro, Kroger and Pinault-Printemps-Redoute, and turned over $1 billion by the end of 2000. They have managed to recruit over 300 suppliers. Retailers pay a fee to join and suppliers are charged a commission if they sell anything through the exchange. The Worldwide Retail Exchange (WWRE), an alternative grouping bringing together mostly US retailers, has now recruited over 50 retail members and expects to turn over $500 billion in 2001. The lesson for suppliers to the retail market is that soon all suppliers will have to join one or more of these marketplaces. Being able to trade online will be a prerequisite to doing business.

Consolidation

Before you rush off and sink all your savings into a B2B marketplace you need to be sure you have found a viable niche. Successful ideas seem to fall into three categories:

1. the horizontal model that can service many markets, like sparesFinder;
2. one type of vertical model where there are just a few suppliers and many buyers; and
3. the other type of vertical market where there are many suppliers and just a few buyers.

Their success depends on recruiting enough members to make it work. As the numbers are ultimately finite there is bound to be some consolidation in the not too distant future. Some commentators say the current crop of 1,400 B2B marketplaces will consolidate into about 400, so site owners need to consider what added-value services they can offer to stay ahead of the rest. It may be that some will specialise in specific geographical areas so that they can provide a quality service. You need to think big though. It is reckoned that any B2B marketplace needs at least £1 billion in turnover to break even, so your chosen market needs to be able to deliver that kind of purchasing power if it is to succeed in the long run.

The most exciting aspect of B2B marketplaces is that they are a new concept born from the new way of looking at buying and selling thanks to the Internet. Virtually anyone can start one, with the right level of funding. The sparesFinder example was funded in four stages with mostly private investors' money of less than £500,000 initially. This is not a huge sum compared with some dot.com start-ups. Even a small business can become a big one with the right idea and the vision to see the mechanics of how it could add value for customers.

E-business action plan	Useful cyber links
Is my big idea actually a B2B marketplace?	www.theecademy.com
Do I have the right industry contacts?	www.taforum.org.uk
Do I have the right computer/management skills?	www.trainingzone.co.uk
Investigate some private investors	www.bestmatch.co.uk

10 Customer relationship management and your database

Let us assume you have a great Internet idea. That you have created a robust Web site. That you are recruiting sufficient customers in your quest for critical mass. That you are starting to make some profit or at least you can see when it will start to come through. You notice that you are getting lots of hits on your site but that your paying customers are relatively low as a percentage of visitors. You start to think that recruiting more customers or getting existing visitors to actually buy is not proving to be so easy.

You have a flash of inspiration. What you really need to do is market to the customers you already have on a planned basis rather than spend all your time constantly search for new ones. This is known as a CRM strategy – a customer relationship management plan. Without one, all your hard work will have been in vain. After all a Web site is actually a direct marketing tool and needs to be developed using direct marketing techniques if it is going to deliver sustainable value in the long run. All good e-businesses start with a Web site designed to capture visitor details.

Web sites designed to reflect the customer

The way a visitor enters your site and goes from page to page and link to link is defined by the architecture of your site. Most Web sites list a series of products or services on the homepage. If you can see what you want listed, you simply click through to the relevant page. However, the more successful sites start from the premise that visitors would rather see a description of themselves first. In other words, successful sites start with the markets the site is aimed at rather than a list of products. After all, many visitors may not really know exactly what they want until they see it. By starting with the needs of the visitor you are embarking on a CRM strategy. David Siegel in his book, *Futurize your Enterprise* (1999), calls this an 'extroverted' site.

But to do the job properly your CRM needs to cover all the different media you use so that customers approaching your business through the traditional media are not treated differently to those who come through your e-business. You must avoid having the same customer categorised differently according to the medium used. This does not give a good impression to customers who expect you to know their habits and status, even though they may now be buying from you in a different way than before.

To provide consistency you need to organise your list of visitors and customers into a common database so that all their browsing and buying activity can be tracked to enable you to serve them better. Take the following case. A customer wants to buy a washing machine. He may have completed a coupon in a magazine and asked for more details. He may then visit a local department store where the departmental manager takes his name to send him a specific brochure. He may then be directed to your Web site by a television advertisement. He looks up your site and places an order online. While waiting for delivery, he is pestered by your telesales team about the coupon he filled in requesting information. The next day the department store rings up to see if he has received the brochure. Four weeks after the washing machine arrives he receives a direct mailshot telling him all about a great new washing machine and that he should pop along to his local department store to see it. This scenario may sound farcical but unless you integrate your enquiries and customer database this is exactly what will happen to your valued site visitors.

The Page & Moy story

Page & Moy Travel is a long-established holiday company with a pedigree stretching back to the 1960s. Over the years it had developed a direct marketing approach to selling holidays that relied on a vast amount of stored data on its past and present customers as well as specific contracts with associations, magazines and clubs.

As a direct travel business with 400 staff and a turnover of almost £50 million, it found itself inundated with paper and brochures. It even had its own print department just to keep up. There was also a supervisory layer of staff who would sit behind the telephone clerks to manage the distribution of new information and train the newcomers. It was a cumbersome arrangement by anyone's standards. In 1996 it decided enough was enough. All its paper files and references would have to be computerised if only to save on the cost of constant photocopying. A graduate trainee with a computer background was given the task of turning all the paper into electronic files and linking everyone through an intranet. All the Lever Arch files disappeared from the desks of all the travel clerks. When a new holiday product or promotion was announced the information would be placed on the intranet to which everyone had access, instead of distributing photocopied announcements. Now staff could compare holiday products for customers 'live' by looking at their desktop screens, often visually split several ways to provide instant comparisons while the customer was still on the phone.

While Page & Moy was developing the screen-based information system it became apparent that it would need real-time links to its holiday product suppliers so that it could check instant availability for

its customers. It decided that the Internet could provide the channel
through which this information could come. Up to this point it still had
no Web site because the system was such that customers received
direct mail or saw an advertisement and rang in to make their booking.
There was no need for one – but it could see there may be a need fairly
soon.

The death of print

Page & Moy's strategy for the previous 30 years had been to get
customers through print-based affiliation (magazine offers, direct mail,
cooperative advertising) but it was becoming clear that the opportunities to reach new print-based markets was disappearing with the rise in
television shopping and the Internet. In 2000 the Travel Channel sold
over 360,000 holidays direct. It was clear that the World Wide Web
was going to be a highly personal medium that could produce much
better conversion ratios than advertising and print, mainly due to being
able to get so much more information about the Internet customer for
later marketing. This provided the commercial imperative to get online
and start developing an electronic channel of communication and
distribution.

Web-framing skills

Page & Moy set up a division called 'epm' (electronic Page & Moy)
which offered customers an up-to-date, online version of its telephone
service. The onscreen brand was called go-nowtravel.com (see the
homepage in Figure 10.1). By linking the site in real time to all
its holiday product suppliers it could offer the most up-to-date availability on the market, thereby offering the widest possible choice. A
Web site was also more content-rich than a brochure. It
could provide much more peripheral information about destinations
through links and could even show hotel rooms in 360-degree presen-
tations.

With its late-offers database stretching to around 20 separate

Figure 10.1 Page & Moy's go-nowtravel.com homepage

suppliers, it could boast over 1 million options during some periods for that section of the market that likes to leave things until the last minute. The next step was to offer holiday services to affiliated groups in the same way it had done so with printed magazines and newspapers, but this time online. BUPA, Safeway (see Figure 10.2) and *The Scotsman* were just a few of the organisations to which it provided a holiday booking service, branded to the client through framing techniques.

All the information collected across the various marketing routes is then channelled into a central database (see Figure 10.3) and provides the registered database for e-mail marketing.

The advantage of migrating the customers in this way from unknown enquiries into known buyers is the enormous saving in future marketing costs. Direct marketing to traditional lists of past customers would cost in the region of £400 per thousand. E-mail messages,

Figure 10.2   The Safeway homepage with the Page & Moy travel deal patch on the right-hand side

highly targeted to the individual even down to what holiday they took the previous year, cost virtually nothing, apart from the servicing cost of the ongoing database.

Keeping customers coming back

All the traditional direct marketing techniques used by Page & Moy in the past are now being revitalised by the database possibilities of the Internet but without the costs. It reckons it is able to offer even better deals to it customers now because of lower marketing costs and, perhaps more crucially, the amount of holiday information you can put on a Web site in comparison with a standard brochure. That means more satisfied customers and a higher rate of repeat bookings. It is now working on WAP (Wireless Application Protocol) enabled techniques

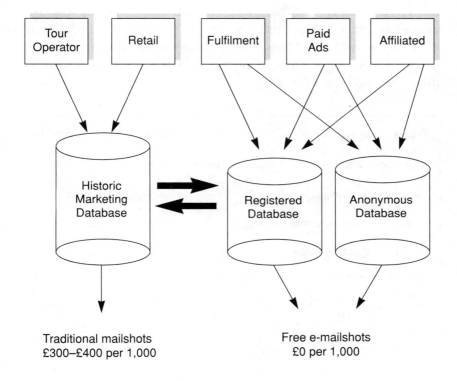

Figure 10.3 E-mailshots

as it feels that mobile commerce will be the way future holidaymakers will book rather than through a fixed PC. Only time will tell whether it is right.

The moral

For many companies, recording customer behaviour electronically can provide perhaps for the first time a highly detailed profile of who buys what and why. This information is vital if your products are to continue to appeal to customers. The database you will develop will also provide a virtually cost-free way to market other products to those customers either through reciprocation or through e-mailings. Your Customer Relationship Management strategy, in other words how you keep your existing visitors or customers coming back, is what will drive your e-business forward.

E-business action plan	Useful cyber links
Make your Web site reflect your customers	www.bC.com
Organise your enquiries efficiently	www.goldmine.com
Plan your customer contact strategy	www.sales.com
Check out CRM software	www.apps.com

11 *From small business to big business*

There is no doubt that the early years of the dot.com revolution have been littered with a number of high profile failures. Some of the losses have been spectacular. Such bad news has always been good news for the newspaper publishing industry – it is always much more entertaining for readers when things go wrong. But there have also been some remarkable success stories that have received less public attention. In many cases profits have yet to come through, but there is no doubt in the minds of their backers that their investments will in time pay off.

Finding the right level of funds at the right time for a budding e-business on an ongoing basis needs to be planned for. It is likely that the funds will not come from the big banks as it has done in the past for most small businesses wishing to expand their business. This chapter is therefore dedicated to what to do if you have a big idea that needs to be financed.

The current trading background for dot.coms

When two twentysomething Cornell University graduates floated Theglobe.com on the New York Stock Exchange in the late 1990s the share price recorded the highest ever one-day rise on Wall Street – 606 per cent. Within 12 months the price had fallen by 98.5 per cent and they were both replaced by a 50-year-old advertising executive.

The tale of high expectations followed by poor sales and dubious management has been repeated in the UK. There is even a Web site dedicated to tracking dot.com failures, although there are rumours, ironically, that this too may be having financial difficulties. The availability of investment funds seems to have receded in line with the absence of any real evidence of future profits. But it need not be the same for every dot.com business by any means. There are still many investors in the marketplace who are keen to back new e-businesses provided there is a convincing business plan.

Developing your e-business plan

Assuming you have a general idea that you are going to need more than you currently have in the bank to fund the development of your e-business, the first thing to consider is the main headings of expenditure over, say, a five-year period:

- Salaries: list all the salaries you will need to pay including any secretarial help and the estimated effects of inflation.
- Benefits: add on all the salary-related extras like National Insurance, cars, expenses, travel, pensions, bonuses, overtime, recruitment fees.
- Marketing: allow for new campaigns and procedures, ongoing Web site development, selling aids, public relations, ASP software, trading licences.

- Distribution: postage or shipping costs, packaging, warehousing, dispatch, returns allowance, stocks and stocks unsold, insurances, taxes if applicable, percentage per country market.
- Central support: finance, legal, human resources, professional advice.
- Equipment: new office hardware, warehousing plant, buildings, cleaning, security, depreciation, servicing/leases.

The easiest way to approach this is to take your normal end-of-year list of costs as drafted by your accountant and complete a similar list for your new e-business. Depending on your market you may have other more specific costs without which you could not trade on the Internet or deliver your customers' orders. The next list is probably several tables showing what sales you expect to generate from various markets and at what margin:

- Sales from the traditional business: static, growing or declining.
- Sales from the e-business: speed of take-up (reasons why), global markets.
- Sales from associates/affiliations/agents.
- Indirect sales from reciprocal site links.

This section will necessarily be estimated, but you should err on the side of caution and if possible give sound evidence as to why you think sales will be at the level stated within each category. It is quite possible that there may be no sales for some time, so you should come clean and say so. An overview of your intended market, with plausible estimates of your share over the first five years, will help to add credibility to your claims that somewhere in all your figures is a viable business.

From this first pass through the planning stages you should be able to draw your own conclusions as to whether you think you have a viable business idea. If you do not believe it, neither will the investors. Case histories and anecdotal evidence may be the only third-party support you can get as to whether what you are proposing will work, but it is worth compiling as there is unlikely to be any other market survey or industry statistics you could use to support your plan. Clearly the most important support you could receive for your plan would be future customers. Research could bring these out in the open, but do not rely too heavily on them as would-be customers can be notoriously fickle as soon as you ask them for money up front to fund your first year.

The business model

Once you have satisfied yourself that what you are attempting could actually return a sustainable profit, you need to articulate your business model in terms simple enough for a non-specialist to understand. You should also provide some evidence that you are ahead of the game in business terms and that your slant on the idea represents the way the market is going within your particular industry niche.

For example, the printing industry is already well advanced in most uses of the Internet so if you are in this field you may wish to highlight that you intend to do things using WAP technology. Or it could be that you supply archaeological site maps to academics but that you would supply them online as 3-D, all-around images. Whatever it is, it needs to add a new dimension to what already exists.

One of the main advantages of any business is its scalability. Could your e-concept be rolled out to many markets around the world, both geographically and across many industries? If so it stands a better chance of attracting development funds. You need to have worked out the estimated numbers of your market, both actual and potential, so that any backers can see the scale of the returns that are possible given the right level of investment.

How easily can your idea be replicated? If it can be, is there any way you can protect it through patents, licences, trading rights or special equipment to protect its growth over the first few years? The technology needs to be bespoke whenever possible so that competitors will not be able to replicate easily what you intend to do.

Is there any way that you can persuade one or two strategic buyers to sign a letter of intent to work with you on an exclusive basis in the early stages? A useful way forward may be to give them some equity options in return for their use of your idea so that you will have at least one big customer even before you launch.

Another way to reduce the risk of early failure is to save cash by leasing rather than buying equipment and going for reciprocal marketing whenever possible rather than large scale brand-building. It goes without saying that excessive salaries and club class air tickets should not be 'policy' in the first few years, if at all. Sentiment has turned away so much from the excessive cash-burners that humility in the business plan can earn you lots of brownie points when the chips are down.

Do you really know who your competitors are and what they charge? It is not uncommon for a new e-business idea to be thought of at around the same time by several people around the world. There can be no copyright on an idea. The key thing is to get your idea to market as soon as possible and build volume. Attend seminars, go to exhibitions, read the trade press and start collecting articles about anything with even a remote connection to your big idea. At worst you could save yourself a great deal of time and effort if you discovered someone else had already done it. At best you might see a fatal flaw in the technical detail of your competitors' plan which, with a bit of tweaking, could propel your idea into a world-beater.

Perhaps the most important aspect of your plan is the senior people who will take day-to-day charge of the business as it grows. They will need to be robust, know their industry, be well connected and get on well together as a team. When it comes to going for funds, the VCs (venture capitalists) will set great store by the maturity of the team and how they interact, as at the end of the day if there is a problem these are the people who are going to have to knuckle down and turn it around. Any evidence you can show that at least one or better still all of you are serial entrepreneurs, the better it will be.

If you can honestly say that you have all the answers to the above questions and lots more detailed analysis besides, you might feel confident enough to then go and look for some venture capital to get your e-business off the ground.

Finding the funds

There are many sources of funds for a business wishing to expand. In theory there is nothing special about e-businesses. The high profile stories about raising millions on the markets are really the tip of a very large iceberg and the vast majority of companies use the traditional routes to raise capital:

- friends and family;
- banks;
- private investors;
- VCs;
- government agencies;
- joint ventures with complementary businesses;
- customer equity partnerships.

Apart perhaps from the friends and family route, these sources will certainly want a detailed business plan and a defensible sales plan on which they can safely make a decision. All your assumptions need to be shown. You should also ensure that there are a number of 'safety factors' built in to the plan so that if things do not grow as fast as you said they would, you have an alternative scenario. Backers are never very keen on being asked for more money at some later stage when things go wrong, so getting your sums right in the first place makes good sense.

A further factor to consider is that your funding can come from a variety of sources; it does not all have to come from a single source. In fact the majority of e-business start-ups have a combination of private investors, founders' money, local grants, some medium-term bank loans and perhaps one longer-term venture capital arrangement. Each of these sources will have different rates attached and different timescales, so your cash flow plan becomes one of the most important business measures you will need to use in the first few years. Government support should not be sniffed at either. Often government agencies are very keen to have a local company 'showing the way' to the rest of the business community and make it relatively easy for you to qualify for grants. Some can be as much as £250,000 or more, which for many e-businesses is more than enough to get you going in the right direction.

Venture capital

Of all the sources of funds, the largest will be either private investors known as 'business angels', or VCs. Private investors may want less return and a longer payback period but may insist on some equity. They will be interested in how they could save tax from their invest-ment, so you need to be prepared to be flexible as to how the invest-ment is brought into the company. They are useful investors to have as they are generally the easiest people to go to if more funds are required at a later stage and are likely to have the least demands in terms of payback periods, if they are convinced you have a good idea.

VCs, on the other hand, tend to be very precise about what they want and when they want it. They will probably have a brochure explaining the type of businesses they want to be involved with and the type of funding they generally provide. They may specialise in start-ups or they may prefer to invest later in the cycle. They could introduce you to complementary business partners with whom they see synergies for your business. Or they might provide the missing technical or people management expertise to complete your senior team. You could do some initial research by logging on to the British Venture Capital Association (www.bvca.co.uk) to see the range of members they represent.

In general they will not be technical experts in your field but they have had a lot of experience of what works and what does not. So, when you are preparing your presentation to send them, you need to be as succinct as possible. Your accountant or solicitor might arrange an introduction to the three or four who would be most likely to look at your plan sympathetically. But unlike dealing with a bank, you are in the driving seat. The VCs will be vying with each other to offer the finance if the plan stands up as viable, so you need to consider carefully each offer you receive and choose the one you think can add value to what you are doing. All of them will be looking for high returns within a three to five year period, so the relationship will not go on for ever, but it would be better to take the funding from people you get on with rather than sacrifice good business empathy for a few less onerous terms.

The VC presentation

If your idea is attractive to the VC they will want to meet you and perhaps one other member of your senior team and have a presentation from you about your e-business. Meetings are normally scheduled for an hour or so. You need to be brief and direct. This is not the time for waxing lyrical about how you started your business 20 years ago in a garden shed. You need to plan your presentation carefully to leave yourself enough time to go through the basic idea and the figures in your plan. No more than a dozen laptop images will be required to get the main ideas across.

In this first session they will give you an opportunity to ask them questions, so prepare what you need to know beforehand and make a careful note of the answers, as you may need to compare what they say with what other VCs tell you. If all goes well you will be invited back for a longer discussion with perhaps an industry expert sitting in and more people from the VC. This session is to help them get a clearer picture of your depth of thinking and for you to see if you could work with the VC on a medium term basis as they will probably want to put one of their own consultants on your board and may even insist that they chair it to protect their investment.

The deal

Depending on the amount of money required, the VC will attach a range of terms and conditions to any funding offered. It will include the percentage of their equity, which will be based on their initial valuation of your new e-business. It will also include how much of the debt you need to repay on an ongoing basis and what happens if you default on any payments. These terms may change if after due diligence they find that your plan is not as watertight as they thought. So, if there is anything negative within the plan or perhaps a market change, you should declare it as soon as you can.

Becoming a dot.com millionaire

Typically, if things go well, your initial funding of, say, £1 million will have been enough to get things going. But a year or so later you find that you need to establish the brand on a national basis to get the real returns. So, you may need to go back and ask for £10 million. Two years later the business model is working well in the UK but you see an opportunity to expand the concept into Europe, so you go back and ask for £30 million. The stage after this could well be a flotation or IPO (Initial Public Offering) after which you may well realise all your initial equity and become a dot.com millionaire.

Afterword

Within the e-business environment the journey from your first networked computer to your first million could be a very short step. There have been some notable success stories in the e-commerce revolution, but there have also been some dreadful disasters. Overvaluations by the stock markets of the world, based on nothing more than scalable concepts, and naïve management, have perhaps given e-business a bad name. Even analysts say that there is now only room for 400 to 500 B2B marketplaces in the world once everyone realises what economies of scale the Internet can deliver. There are currently over 1,400 trying to make a profit.

To be a world leader in any sphere takes a certain amount of courage. As a small business owner the occasional loss is part of business life. But you have to have the right temperament to cope with managing losses in the millions. StepStone, the pan-European online recruitment company, recently reported quarterly losses in the region of £25 million. When they floated, shares were issued to investors at 241 pence each. By the end of 2000 they were valued at just 160 pence. At the time the management were confident their spending had peaked and that from now on they were on the path to profit. Coping with the pressure of managing losses is not for the faint-hearted.

For every huge business with global pretensions there are many thousands of smaller businesses that can grow and prosper using exactly the same technology and delivery systems as those multi-nationals who seem to dominate the headlines. Size is no longer the big advantage it used to be. Global reach is now available to anyone with a link to the World Wide Web and you do not have to spend millions to make a profit. Nor do you have to use every innovation that comes along. Take what works for your business rather than have everything foisted on you by 'experts'. You can become profitable within months, if you take it step by step.

Throughout this book I have used examples of companies both big and small using the existing new technology to great effect. But speed of change is the defining factor of the Internet age. Almost all of the examples quoted are still using fixed landlines to send data to distant parts of the network.

I recently attended a presentation to would-be e-business entrepreneurs at Microsoft's UK headquarters in Reading. The introduction was a short video that demonstrated a world some time in the future in which m-commerce or mobile commerce would be the technology to dominate the next phase of the information revolution. In 1995 there were just 8 million mobile phone users across the world. By the end of the century there were 450 million. The average business person or even consumer for that matter is more likely to want to communicate through a mobile facility in the years to come than to be dependent on a static, desktop PC. WAP is the future, it would appear, in virtually every industry you can name.

It is likely that the e-business start-ups of the future will have to be thinking about using mobile telephony technology as a strategic part of their new product or service if the idea is going to survive the critical first few years. The challenge is therefore one of constant change and adaptation to the new advances being made. If you can work these new changes into your unique e-business idea to gain that competitive edge, you stand to increase your chances of success... until another advance is made. Dealing with those changes will not be easy. But no one ever said running a business would be easy, Internet or no Internet.

John G Fisher, 2001
E-mail: motivcon@aol.com

References

Deloitte & Touche (2000) E-Business: Challenges and opportunities for growth companies, *Real Business*, Caspian Publishing Ltd, London, March, p 27

Grossman, W M (2000) Achieve Immediate Profits With Your Dot.com Start-up, *Executive Intelligence*, **1**, June/July, pp 8–9

Harpin, S (ed) (2000) *Kick-Starter.com*, Chapter 8: Legal aspects of setting up an Internet business, Macmillan Press, Basingstoke

Hewson, David (2000) A Tiddler Fish Shop Grows Big in the Vast Waters of the Net, *The Sunday Times*, 5 March, p 13

Jupiter Media Matrix (2000) article in *Executive Intelligence*, **2**, Sept/Oct (original survey published by Publicis Blueprint, Wokingham on behalf of 3com (www.3com.co.uk/active-business))

Papows, J (1999) *Enterprise.com*, Nicholas Brealey Publishing, London

SAS Institute (2000) *Turning E-Commerce Into E-Profit*, SAS Institute, p 2

Siegel, D (1999) *Futurize Your Enterprise*, John Wiley & Sons Inc, New York

Wapshott, T (2000) The Bumpy Road to Freedom, *The Times*, 24 October (an article about ISP providers)

Index